AGITPOP

AGITPOP

Political Culture
and Communication Theory

Arthur Asa Berger

Transaction Publishers
New Brunswick (U.S.A.) and London (U.K.)

Copyright © 1990 by Transaction Publishers,
New Brunswick, New Jersey 08903

Library of Congress Catalog Number: 89-35247
ISBN: 0-88738-315-7
Printed in the United States of America

Library of Congress Cataloging-in-Publication Data
Berger, Arthur Asa, 1933–
   Agitpop : political culture and communication theory.
      p.   cm.
   ISBN 0-88738-315-7
   1. Political culture.   2. Communication.   3. Information the-
ory.
   I. Title.
   JA75.7.B47   1989
   306.2—dc20   89-35247
                                                          CIP

In memory of Mulford G. Sibley

Contents

Acknowledgments

Aaron Wildavsky's seminal work on political culture provided the framework for this book. I find his ideas extremely suggestive and in this book I "carry the ball" (to adopt a football metaphor) "snapped" to me by Aaron. He was also kind enough to review my chapter on politics and communication theory and make a number of helpful suggestions, for which I am most grateful.

I also benefitted greatly from Irving Louis Horowitz's recommendation that I add material on communication theory to my manuscript. It originally contained an introduction, explaining Wildavsky's ideas about the four political cultures found in complex societies, and eight chapters on television programs, media events, films, and related subjects.

Adding material on communication theory made a great deal of sense, because I needed to offer readers a theoretical base to support my analyses. It also provided me with an opportunity to offer my readers some new theoretical work I've done. The fact that I've written on communication theory may be a surprise to a number of people who seem to believe that there's no theory behind my work—that I am both data free and theory free, and of course, in the best social-scientific tradition, value free.

In the last chapter of this book I offer a long autobiographical statement (perhaps "confessional" is a better term) dealing with my work and the theory behind it. To paraphrase St. Augustine, "to San Francisco came I, burning, burning," in 1965. Since then I've spent a good deal of time, to tip Matthew Arnold upside down, examining the worst that men (and women) have thought and said.

In addition, I owe a debt of gratitude to my students, who have played a game I developed using Aaron Wildavsky's ideas—which I call, fittingly, "Aaron Wildavsky." (It probably is closer to being an exercise and will not give such games as *Monopoly* or *Trump* anything to worry about.) The students came up with some extremely interesting ideas. You will be able to read about the fruits of their labors in the first chapter of this book.

Finally, let me express my appreciation to the people at Transaction, whose high degree of professionalism and good humor have made working with them such a great pleasure.

Introduction

I coined the term *agitpop* to focus attention on the political aspects of popular culture and the mass media. The term derives from agitprop, the bureau of agitation and propaganda created by the Russian Communists to spread Marxist ideology through films, plays, and other works of art.

Suggesting that popular culture has a political significance to it is not a startling insight, but it is one that has escaped some. Many scholars are aware of media and popular culture—how could one not be—but not particularly interested in it, considering it beneath contempt, trivial, stupid, and banal—all of which it frequently is.

In the past, much of what I've written about popular culture has been random—in the sense that it was not grounded in any theory that tied it to social and political matters except in rather vague and general terms. In this book I analyze a number of texts and other examples of popular culture and show how they relate to a theory of political culture articulated by my good friend Aaron Wildavsky.

Wildavsky suggests that people in all complex societies must find the answer to two basic questions: "Who am I?" (to what group do I belong) and "What should I do?" (what rules should I obey). This leads, he explains, to four political cultures, which he identifies as "hierarchical elitist," "competitive individualist," "egalitarian," and "fatalistic." I explain these matters in considerable detail in the first chapter.

The question I try to answer in the first part of this book is "what texts (works) from the mass media and popular culture would members of each of these political cultures be drawn to and find supportive?" I have selected two texts for each political culture, texts that presumably reflect the basic values and beliefs that members of each political culture would have.

I am, to a great degree, a textual analyst or critic and have focused my attention on specific programs or series or films, rather than talking in generalities about the media—though there is some of that in *Agitpop*, also. Thus I have analyzed football and the Iran-Contra hearings in my chapters reflecting hierarchical elitism, dealt with MTV and the human potential movement in my chapters reflecting competitive individualism, analyzed Jewish humor and *Max Headroom* in my chapters reflecting egalitarianism, and written about professional wrestling and *The Terminator* in my chapters reflecting the fatalist orientation.

How these texts relate to each of the four political cultures is a complex question that is considered in the various chapters. I chose subjects that I thought were interesting and revealing and covered a number of different areas. Thus, the chapters deal with a sport, a political media event, humor, a new television genre, a life-style, a satirical television series, wrestling, and a film. In principle, of course, anything could be used, but I feel that the subjects I chose were particularly applicable to the matter at hand.

The second part of the book contains chapters on communication theory. One chapter deals with the relationship between Wildavsky's theory and with semiotics and communication, in general. Another essay considers the focal points one might deal with in analyzing media and has a logical structure to it that is, I think, quite elegant. The content is another matter.

I am, I've recently recognized, very binary. I create well-defined structures and operate in a very loose, free-form manner within them. I also write in two different styles: one is straightforward and essentially academic and the other is eccentric and zany. The last chapter is a case in point. It is an autobiographical statement (confessional?) on my identity as a pop culturist, my work, and my various interests and preoccupations. Some might say hang-ups and neuroses? Psychoses?

This chapter has a different tone than the rest of the book, one that is much more reflective of my personality than the first part. This chapter has wordplay and is full of admittedly wild ideas. I sometimes write in a formal and serious way about ideas that seem (are?) quite absurd and ridiculous. I would argue that my methods are those of the Zen masters, who took on the persona of clowns and used humor for their various purposes.

I would hope that *Agitpop* will play a useful role in introducing some readers, especially those who are not political scientists, to Aaron Wildavsky's ideas and their utility in analyzing popular culture and the mass media. For those who find his ideas stimulating and suggestive, let me suggest a volume I edited on his work, *Political Culture and Public Opinion,* also published by Transaction Publishers.

Part One

POLITICAL CULTURE

Collective representations are the result of an immense co-operation, which stretches out not only into space but into time as well; to make them, a multitude of minds have associated, united and combined their ideas and sentiments; for them, long generations have accumulated their experience and their knowledge. A special intellectual activity is therefore concentrated in them which is infinitely richer and complexer than that of the individual. From that one can understand how the reason has been able to go beyond the limits of empirical knowledge. It does not owe this to any vague, mysterious virtue but simply to the fact that according to the well-known formula, man is double. There are two beings in him: an individual being which has its foundation in the organism and the circle of whose activities is therefore strictly limited, and a social being which represents the highest reality in the intellectual and moral order that we can know by observation—I mean society. This duality of our nature has as its consequence in the practical order, the irreducibility of a moral ideal to a utilitarian motive, and in the order of thought, the irreducibility of reason to individual experience. In so far as he belongs to society, the individual transcends himself, both when he thinks and when he acts.

—*Emile Durkheim,* The Elementary Forms of the Religious Life

1

Political Culture and Popular Culture: Predicting Preferences or Magister Aaron— The Wildavsky Game

Popular Culture and Political Preferences

There is a great deal of controversy over what popular culture is and isn't. In a previous essay I asked "Why is popular culture so unpopular?" and came to the conclusion that popular culture is a convenient tool for elites to castigate the masses. Since it is not acceptable to say nasty things about the lower classes or various subcultures nowadays, elites get rid of the hostility they feel towards these people by saying nasty things about their taste.

Popular culture, the public arts, mass culture—whatever you want to call it—is very popular with the general public, the common man and woman (and adolescent and child), who consume incredible amounts of it as they watch television programs, go to the movies, attend baseball and football games, read romances, eat at fast food joints, wear the latest fashions, and so on.

It is possible to distinguish between the mass media, which bring us a great deal of what we commonly describe as popular culture, and the various genres—kinds of programs or films that these media carry (and shape, since the medium, while it may not be the message, certainly has an impact on it). A great deal of popular culture is mass-mediated, but there are other aspects of popular culture that are not, though they may be affected by the mass media and, in particular, the institution of advertising.

There is even a question, in the minds of many scholars, as to whether the distinction between popular culture and other kinds of culture—in particular, unpopular or "elite" culture—means anything. There certainly is a difference between watching a rock bank on television and attending a poetry reading. But what if that poetry reading is on television and thousands of people watch it? Or millions of people?

It may very well be that popular culture and elite culture (to take the two extremes) are not that different and the valorization of elite culture by elites is a matter of their attempting to find a way to differentiate themselves from others. It provides what we might call "cultural distance" to go along with "social distance." Frequently, however, elite elements in society often find themselves involved with popular culture—watching football on television or reading the comics in the newspapers. Do we find here a distinction without a difference?

Media sometimes graduate, so to speak, from being popular to being elite—that is, capable of generating "serious" works of art that so-called cultivated types take seriously. Thus, the French "discovered" film and it changed from being considered a kind of trivial medium to a very important one. (The French also rescued Faulkner from being considered an unimportant regional writer to being recognized as a great, world-class writer. When the French tell us that comics or football are important art forms, no doubt we will see new things in them, as well. Some American intellectuals draw the line at Jerry Lewis, but I suspect they will come around eventually.)

The topic I am investigating here involves the relationship that exists between the four political cultures that we find in complex societies (according to Aaron Wildavsky) and the various kinds of popular culture found in American society. Is it possible to predict which television programs, sports, foods, drinks, and other aspects of popular culture will be favored by each of the political cultures found in America?

Before I discuss this subject, let me say something about Wildavsky's work on political cultures in democratic societies.

Wildavsky on Political Cultures in Complex Societies

Wildavsky has argued, in a number of books and papers, that there are four basic political cultures found in all complex societies. (See

"Conditions for Pluralist Democracy or Pluralism Means More than One Political Culture in a Country," 1982; and "Choosing Preferences by Constructing Institutions: A Cultural Theory of Preference Formation," undated.) He sets the stage for explaining what the four political cultures are like by discussing cultural theory:

> The dimensions of cultural theory are based on answers to two questions: "Who am I?" and "How Should I Behave?" The question of identity may be answered by saying that individuals belong to a strong group, a collective, that makes decisions binding on all members or that their ties to others are weak in that their choices bind only themselves. The question of action is answered by responding that the individual is subject to many or few prescriptions, a free spirit or one that is tightly constrained.

Thus we find two considerations of utmost importance: whether group boundaries are strong or weak and whether prescriptions are few or many. There are, Wildavsky asserts "only a limited number of cultures that between them categorize most human relations," and this limited number turns out to be four (undated, 7).

These four political cultures are found in figure 1.1, which shows how they relate to one another according to the two basic categories: boundaries and prescriptions. This figure, created by Wildavsky, is adopted from a work by Mary Douglas, *Natural Symbols*, and a collaboration between Douglas and Wildavsky, *Risk and Culture*.

The figure yields four political cultures found in complex societies: *individualism, egalitarianism, collectivism,* and *fatalism.*

Wildavsky has changed his terminology a bit over the years, he used to use the terms "hierarchical collectivism," "competitive individual-

FIGURE 1.1
Models of Four Cultures

Number and Variety of Prescriptions	Strength of Group Boundaries	
	Weak	Strong
Numerous and varied	Apathy (Fatalism)	Hierarchy (Collectivism)
Few and similar	Competition (Individualism)	Equality (Egalitarianism)

Source: Adapted from Douglas 1970; 1982.

ism, "egalitarian sectarianism," and "fatalism." I mention this because in my discussion of a game or exercise that I have played with my students using the Wildavsky formulation, I use the older terminology.

He explains how the four groups form and how they are related to one another, as follows:

> Strong groups with numerous prescriptions that vary with social roles combine to form hierarchical collectivism. Strong groups whose members follow few prescriptions form an egalitarian culture, a shared life of voluntary consent, without coercion or inequality. Competitive individualism joins few prescriptions with weak boundaries, thereby encouraging ever new combinations. When groups are weak and prescriptions strong, so that decisions are made for them by people on the outside, the controlled culture is fatalistic. (Wildavsky, undated, p. 8)

All of these groups need each other, and none is viable on its own, though each group believes its values should be universalized. Hierarchical types need people below them to "sit on top of" and fatalists need "an external source of control to tell them what to do." In the same manner, "egalitarians need something—unfair competition, inequitable hierarchy, nonparticipant fatalists—to criticize," and competitive individualists need the law of contract to fall back on and be "above negotiating."

Sounding more and more like a structural anthropologist and semiologist, he explains, "Conflict among cultures is a precondition of cultural identity. It is the differences and distances from others that define one's own cultural identity" (undated, p. 9).

How the Political Cultures Solve Problems

In order to be viable, every political culture must have ways of dealing with challenges and problems and maintaining social order. In his paper, "Conditions for Pluralist Democracy or Cultural Pluralism Means More than One Political Culture in a Country," written in May, 1982, Wildavsky deals with such matters as: leadership, controlling envy, assigning blame, dealing with inequality, allocating scarce resources, and confronting uncertainty to cite some of the more important topics. Each of these political cultures deals with the phenomena in ways that are congruent with its basic principles and the ways in which they relate to boundaries and prescriptions. As an example of how this works, I will explain how the four political cultures deal with leadership, order, and envy.

Hierarchical collectivism imposes order through the division of labor and argues that inequality is (presumably natural and) of central importance in maintaining the collective. This is done by convincing each element to sacrifice for the good of the whole. Hierarchical collectivism controls envy by limiting ostentation for public events or collective bodies, such as the church or the state, and by emphasizing sacrificial behavior on the part of the leaders. We find, then, a sense of noblesse oblige on the part of those on the top of the hierarchy, who gain loyalty by producing results for those at the bottom.

The competitive individualists see things quite differently. They use contract and mutual agreement as the basis for establishing order and leadership is, like everything else, a function of bargaining and bidding. Leadership is also not seen as universal but connected to specific matters and interests. The competitive individualists do not have a problem with envy, since failure is personalized and not blamed on the system but on individual incapacity. What is crucial in this system is that it is individuals, also, who benefit from the rewards of transactions, which means that they see risk as opportunity. People with this philosophy define freedom as lack of restraints and accept ostentation since everyone, in theory, had the same chance to be successful.

When we come to the egalitarians, leadership is suspect and leaders tend to be charismatic figures who, by force of personality, gather a group of followers around them. The beliefs of the egalitarians are opposite to those of the hierarchical collectivists; egalitarians work to minimize differences between people in every area. When there are problems in a society, the egalitarians tend to blame "the system" and various institutions which are not functioning properly. They are distrustful of authority, but unlike the individualists, who want to promote individual differences, the egalitarians want to diminish individual differences. The style of the egalitarians is common and lowly, and they emphasize equality of result in government, arguing that people have common needs for which government must accept responsibility.

Wildavsky argues that the hierarchical collectivists (who, we might say, "generate order") and the competitive individualists (who, we might say, "generate economic growth") form "the establishment" and that the egalitarians form what might be called an antiestablishment, and function as critics of the establishment.

The last group, the fatalists, are for all practical purposes outside of the political order and participate in it only minimally. They exercise little control over their lives, and see power as external to them. They are not envious (since they believe in luck or fate) and see themselves as victims in a system that is capricious and, perhaps, unfair, but which they cannot change.

Wildavsky argues that egalitarians (he calls them "egalitarian sectarians" in his 1982 paper) cannot rule because in large groups, they are inherently unstable—they require "virtually complete consent" (something like the Polish Parliament), which is impossible to maintain when there are large numbers of people. Therefore he argues that "it takes two to tango but three to make a democracy" (1982). While the egalitarians cannot rule effectively, they are needed to offer criticism and make their presence felt. He writes "Given the attraction of opposites, a multi-cultural regime will involve relationships between the establishment and a sectarian culture that can neither rule nor be eliminated. And this, it so happens, is a basic condition for pluralist democracy. (1982)"

This discussion offers a brief overview of Wildavsky's ideas about political cultures—enough so you can understand the relevance of his ideas to the game I have my students play in one of my classes, which we might describe as a game involving political culture and popular culture.

Playing Aaron Wildavsky

I have taught a course called "Analysis of the Public Arts" which deals with the techniques of criticizing popular culture and analyzing the relationship that exists between popular culture and society. The person who created the course used the term "public arts" because it avoided some of the negative connotations of the term "popular," a matter which suggests that certain hierarchical collectivist attitudes seem to be dominant in the academy and society at large.

I teach the course by dealing with four of the principle modes of analyzing popular culture (and elite culture): semiotic theory, psychoanalytic theory, Marxist theory, and sociological theory. We play "Aaron Wildavsky" in the part of the course that deals with Marxist theory, since his model involves political phenomena.

The game is played as follows: I explain to the class, briefly, the basic aspects of Wildavsky's theory (the theory is also dealt with in a small book of media games, activities, simulations and exercises I have written and self-published for the course). Then I divide the class up into groups of three students and ask them to fill out a form in the games book which lists various popular culture topics and asks students to predict how each political culture would relate to each topic. I ask them, for example, to deal with such matters as songs, television shows, films, magazines, books, heroes, games, etc. What they are required to do is predict (or guess) which songs, television programs, films, magazines, etc. would be popular with members of each of the four political cultures.

The game is based on the assumption that individuals (and groups as well) want to avoid dissonance and obtain support for their beliefs and values. Thus, they will seek out popular culture that reinforces their views and avoid popular culture that attacks or somehow calls into question their views. There is good reason to believe that people respond this way to the media and popular culture and are attracted to films, television shows, etc. that are congruent with their beliefs and values. There is enough popular culture around for these groups to have a considerable amount of latitude in finding popular culture that they can relate to, so it is assumed that they actually have the opportunity to make choices. (Even the fatalists have a measure of control here.)

After the students spend a half hour or so working on the charts, we put their findings on the blackboard and have a general discussion of their findings. All members of the class participate in deciding which choices seem to be the best (in terms of reflecting the salient aspects of the political culture most accurately). There is frequently a good deal of hilarity during this discussion and, fittingly, for an egalitarian activity, it sometimes becomes a rather chaotic twenty or thirty minutes. The laughter is caused by the appropriateness of the matches that are made by clever students, who find films or television shows or sports or whatever that are surprisingly meaningful.

As a result of teaching this course many times in recent years, I've been able to collect a sizable number of filled-out political culture charts, which I've saved. I offer a composite table in which I've put together what, in my estimation, is a consensus view.

Table from the Wildavsky Games Analysis

There are, of course, many different entries that could be made for each category, and frequently there was a considerable amount of discussion about which entries were best. On the other hand, in certain cases, there were entries that the class felt were outstanding and which just about everyone accepted.

In the case of songs, for example, there were numerous entries for the hierarchical collectivism category that people felt were acceptable, but there was widespread consensus that *I Did it My Way* was the entry

TABLE 1.1
Consensus View of Wildavsky Game

Topic Analyzed	Hierarchical Collectivism	Competitive Individualism	Egalitarian	Fatalism
Songs	*God Save the Queen*	*I Did It My Way*	*We are the World*	*Anarchy In The UK*
TV Shows	*MacNeil/Lehrer Newshour*	*Dynasty Dallas*	*The Equalizer*	*A-Team*
Films	*Top Gun The Right Stuff*	*Color of Money*	*Woodstock*	*Rambo*
Magazines	*Architectural Digest*	*Money*	*Mother Jones*	*Soldier of Fortune*
Books	*The Prince*	*Looking Out For Number One*	*I'm Okay You're Okay*	*1984*
Heroes	Reagan	Iacocca	Gandhi	Jim Jones
Heroines	Queen Elizabeth	Alexis (Joan Collins)	Mother Teresa	Madonna
Games	Chess	Monopoly	New Games	Russian Roulette
Sports	Football Polo	Tennis	Frisbee	Roller Derby
Fashion	Uniforms	Three piece Suit	Jeans	Thrift Store

that epitomized the competitive individualistic ethos. In the same manner, there was consensus that *Dynasty* and *Dallas* (and the evening soaps, in general) were the best entries for that category under television. We could not get any agreement about which television program fit best under the hierarchical category. The *MacNeil Lehrer Newshour* was chosen by many who felt it was the kind of program "elites" would watch and, perhaps, identify with.

There was also pretty strong consensus in choosing *Money* as the magazine for competitive individualists, *Mother Jones* as the magazine for egalitarians, and *Soldier of Fortune*, a survivalist journal, as the magazine for fatalists. Choosing films is always a problem because students often don't know the older films and tend to make their selections from relatively recent films. The same applies to most of the other categories, as well. It would be interesting to have middle-aged people play the game to see the results. I imagine that their selections would be different and that many older films, television programs, and other works would be chosen. This involves the matter of what we might call *popular cultural literacy*, which I will discuss shortly.

In the books category, the students liked *Looking out for Number One* for individualism and *I'm Okay, You're Okay* for egalitarians. Some suggested the works of Ayn Rand for individualism, which the class liked. But there was little sense that any particular book was the best possible choice for the other categories. In certain cases there were texts that might be classified as the best possible choice. In the category of games, there was widespread agreement about *Monopoly* for competitive individualism and New Games (in which there were no winners or losers) for egalitarianism. And there was a particular sense that Russian roulette was the perfect choice for fatalist games.

We might distinguish between acceptable or good choices and, in certain cases, perfect choices—ones that everyone felt fitted particularly well and showed imagination and even wit. That would explain why, in the case of the perfect choices, students often laughed and expressed amusement over the selection. *My Way*, Russian roulette, and other quintessential examples were seen as inspired and remarkable discoveries. That is, the fit between the values and beliefs of the particular political culture and the text that reflected these values and beliefs was so good that the students couldn't imagine finding anything better.

There are several things that intrigue students about the game. First, there is the problem of finding the right text for each topic and political culture. There are an incredible number of songs, television programs, films, and other texts to choose from, but it is not always easy to find the most appropriate item. Second, there is the element of the puzzle in the game. There are a chart and various categories and a pressure for closure, for finding the right items (similar to the desire for closure felt in filling out crossword puzzles). In addition, there is the game element in this activity—it is seen as something that is fun, something that has a humorous element to it, involving "putting people in their place."

Sometimes when I play the game I use a different form—one that allows the students to choose their own categories, after they have filled out the form with the ones I give them. They are extremely creative in selecting categories and examples, and have done everything from sexual positions to drugs of choice.

Problems with Playing "Aaron Wildavsky"

There are a number of problems with the game—or, to be more specific, with trying to figure out how to make sense of the results of the game. For one thing, we cannot be certain that people in the different political cultures will follow the logic of their values and let it determine their choice of popular culture. Still, as I have suggested, the twin forces of dissonance-avoidance and the desire for reinforcement must be operative, to a certain extent.

There is also the matter of the various films, television programs, and other texts. The game forces us to put a particular text in a specific niche, but it is unlikely that we will find texts that are as focused and ideologically pure as we are forced to make them. Media scholars realize now that different people see a given text in different ways, so there are problems with categorizing any given example of popular culture as being "fatalist" or whatever. On the other hand, there are some cases (*My Way*, Russian roulette, *Dynasty*, etc.) in which there is a rather obvious ideological stance reflected in the texts so that categorizing them as fatalist or egalitarian or whatever does not seem to be too reductionistic.

A problem that continually comes up involves misinterpreting the four political cultures. In some cases the students don't think about the complexities behind the political cultures and this leads to mistaken, or highly problematical, choices of texts. This may be due, in part, to time constraints and my inability to explain Wildavsky's analysis of each of the political cultures adequately. (I might point out, in passing, that the game is not seen as based on class, per se. Some of the competitive individualists may be much wealthier than hierarchical collectivists. I have another game, "class consciousness," which we also play, which deals with socio-economic class and popular culture.)

There is also the matter of preferences. Are preferences of each of the political cultures mutually exclusive? Are there four more or less discrete audiences who pick and choose from what is available on the basis of their tastes (without realizing, of course, that their tastes have been shaped by their political culture) or is there one vast, undifferentiated audience in America (and abroad, where *Dallas* has been extremely popular)? Or, to take up a theme mentioned earlier, is it possible that people from the four different political cultures find elements in just about any given popular culture text that support their view of things?

One topic which the game doesn't address involves the matter of genres. Are certain genres more appealing to particular political cultures than others? Is the detective story, featuring the private eye who is in competition with the police (read "governmental bureaucracy" here) something that competitive individualists find compelling and particularly attractive? My students have already indicated that evening soaps, such as *Dynasty* and *Dallas*, are such. Which political culture would find the morning soaps particularly appealing? Or James Bond movies?

A Note on Popular Cultural Literacy

One thing that I discovered from this game is that my students have an incredible amount of information about the contemporary popular culture scene, and some of them know a great deal about the popular culture of the recent and distant past. When we talk about cultural literacy, then, and bemoan the shocking facts about our students' lack of knowledge about U.S. history or our leaders, we are generally talking about matters relating to what might be described as elite culture.

I would imagine that our students have had endless history courses in which they learned the dates of our wars and who Franklin Delano

Roosevelt was, but this information seems to have entered one ear and immediately exited the other one, in part because it was defined as "schoolwork" and, for one reason or another (perhaps because of the way history is taught?) of no interest to the students. Curiously, students are able to remember all kinds of details about our popular culture, so I would suggest our lamentable lack of cultural literacy is somewhat restricted. Our young people (and some of our not-so-young people) may not know the names of anyone on the Supreme Court but they probably know the names of everyone who has ever been a member of The Supremes and the names of endless numbers of rock stars, movie stars, baseball players, and football players.

The problem is that many people tend to devalue this information and thus define our young people as culturally illiterate. This labelling reminds me of the days when we thought there were people who were lacking culture or were culturally deprived. We now recognize that everyone has culture; it is just that we (that is, our elites and opinion leaders) didn't recognize some of these cultures as "valid" or think they were worth very much.

Conclusions

What playing "Political Cultures and Popular Culture" suggests, ultimately, is that there is an ideological content to our popular culture, even though we may not always recognize that such is the case. (I would argue, further, that the people who create this popular culture generally have no sense that they are creating works with ideological dimensions to them.) Whether this ideological content is the critical issue in determining how people choose the popular culture they like, and what impact this ideological content has on the general public and the body politic, is something that demands serious attention.

Thus, the game of "Aaron Wildavsky" may have a humorous or frivolous aspect to it, but like all humor, which finds ways of speaking truth to or about power, it is connected to matters of great importance.

Ideal characteristics of football players, as of success-oriented businesspeople, include hard work, diligence, dedication, and denial of individual self-interest for the good of the team ("teamwork"). But, the anthropologists argue, rewards for such behavior in business are not always forthcoming. Because of the complicated and often capricious nature of decision making within larger organizations, workers are not always assured that they will be rewarded for their dedication and good work. For precisely this reason football is popular. Any fan can, through careful study and observation, become an expert on the rules, teams, scores, individual statistics, and patterns of play in football.

Even more important, football demonstrates to fans that the values stressed by business really do pay off. Teams whose players and coaches work hardest, show the most team spirit, and best develop and coordinate the talents of the players can be expected to win more often than others. Classic capitalist values, which are still presented as guides for success in American business, are represented by and affirmed through football. Football is popular therefore because it is so well suited to the American economy, society, and traditional values.

   —*Conrad Kottak,* Researching American Culture

2

Theses on the Game of Football

Explanation of the Enterprise

What follows are a series of speculations about the game of football. It is an extremely complicated sport, embedded deeply in the American economy (as a gigantic business), the media (as the content of much radio and television), and the American psyche (in that it provides us, for example, with all manner of heroes and with an outlet for our aggressive feelings). What I have tried to do, in each of the segments that follows, is look beyond the immediate topic and find philosophical, psychoanalytic, ideological, or some other kind of significance.

My thesis is that while football, on one level, is just a sport that provides entertainment for millions of fans, at a deeper level (and perhaps beyond the level of awareness most of the time) it has other meanings and speaks to us in different ways. This is a speculative enterprise I have embarked on, something like throwing a "long bomb"—and I would like to think that as in football, high risks sometimes lead to big gains. On the other hand, sometimes you take a chance and it doesn't work out well at all. I assume a familiarity with the game and an openness to interpretations that may seem individualistic if not eccentric.

When I was in my mid-twenties and in the army in Washington, D.C., I wrote high school sports for *The Washington Post*. As a scholar I've always found football curiously compelling, even though games are often dull. But for every boring game there are those that are fabulously exciting, in which the final outcome is not determined until the last few seconds of the game. I am, by occupation, a professor of communications and my speciality is popular culture. Thus, when *I* watch football on television I am doing research; when *you* watch football on television, on the other hand, you are merely wasting time. With that understood, let us begin.

Escape and Containment.

Although football is a game about gaining territory and scoring points, ultimately football is about escape and containment. Much of the language is about this matter. We talk about ends being "free" or backs "finding space" or "finding running room," and one of the great thrills in the game is watching a back break free and make a long run.

In this respect, the game can be seen as a metaphor for life in American society—and society in general, though it is only in America and Canada that the game is played with any regularity. The defensive team represents, to carry the analogy along, the institutions of society that exist (as we tend to define matters) to inhibit us and punish us when we transgress. We realize that we are not social atoms; we need our team to help us, but we long for those special moments when we are free, when we have left the last defensive player behind and we can run to glory.

Sigmund Freud wrote a book titled *Civilization and Its Discontents*, in which he argued that the price we pay for becoming civilized is repression, especially of our sexual drives. Thus, this desire for freedom and for escaping containment is a means of gaining a bit of release from all the rules and regulations that we must observe. Without society and culture we are little more than animals; with society and culture we are repressed. And that is why "breaking free," if only for a moment and if only in a game, means so much to us.

Strategy or the Power of Mind

Although the game of football is a rough and violent one, played by huge and often very powerful players, it really is based on strategy and the power of mind. Much of the time in a football game is spent in huddles, in which players decide on the particular play they will use for the next down. It is amazing to think that young men who may find it hard to pass a course can remember many very complicated plays and execute them with precision.

It has been estimated that the ball is actually in play (that is, someone is running with the ball or passing it or kicking it) something like eight or ten minutes during the typical game. The rest of the time is spent huddling or in time outs, talking with the coaches at the sidelines, or, after the play, returning to the huddle.

Coaches attain notoriety on the basis of their ability to create a team (that is, choose good players) and strategize—come up with a good "game plan." In the San Francisco Bay area, where I live, the coach of the San Francisco 49ers, Bill Walsh, is sometimes referred to as a genius because of his ability to develop game plans and develop great quarterbacks.

Communication or the Importance of Information

If you watch a football game, quite likely you will see that the head coaches are wired up with electronic gear, so they can be in constant communication with the spotters who are high up in the stands, in the press box, or around it, where they can get the big picture and relay information about formations back to the head coach. On the basis of this information, the coach sometimes revises his plans.

What is crucial, then, is the role of information in the game. Information plays a part in all sports, but think of the difference, for example, between football and baseball. The manager of the baseball team is not wired up and does his decision making from the field because there is no need to worry about special formations. The information is passed via signals made by coaches. Catchers also pass information about the kind of pitch they want by using signals, but the whole matter is much simpler and more primitive than in football, where formations vary with each play.

Football mirrors contemporary American society, in which information has come to play an increasingly major role. Some scholars have described contemporary America as an information society, in that more than fifty percent of the gross national product comes from services and the information area, rather than from manufacturing. Information is what makes it possible to decide on strategy and communication is what facilitates all this.

Mistakes and the Role of Chance

One of the things we learn from football is that human beings are fallible and prone to making errors. It is this propensity for screwing up that energizes the game and makes it dramatic. The coaches make their perfect plans and then watch, on the sidelines, as kickers shank balls, punt receivers drop passes, quarterbacks overthrow their receivers, and runners fumble and give up the ball. Quite often, teams beat themselves with their own mistakes, and coaches can only pace back and forth on the sidelines and tear their hair out.

Of course, mistakes occur on both sides, usually, so they tend to cancel one another out, though some teams seem to be more disciplined and error free than others, and the teams that make fewer errors tend to be more successful than teams that make many errors. So we learn, from watching football, that mistakes are part of life and that we must factor them into the scheme of things. Rather than getting upset over them and becoming immobilized, we have to expect to make errors ourselves and to hope that our opponents will also make errors.

The irony is that we read a great deal about all the training that the players endure and see that there are legions of coaches on every team, yet despite all this training, players—being human beings—screw up constantly. The function of coaches, then, is not to eliminate errors but to minimize them. Any enterprise that involves humans, football teaches us, will be permeated with mistakes, which means that football ultimately liberates us from any sense that we must, somehow, be perfect and never make mistakes. From a psychoanalytic point of view, this aspect of football is beneficial.

Penalties and the Role of Authority

Football, like all games, has many rules, and to make certain that the rules are followed and the game is fair, there are umpires and referees who have the power to punish teams by assessing penalties for various transgressions. It is assumed that authority is valid and while the referees may also make mistakes, since human beings are all bumblers and prone to make errors, the decisions of the umpires and referees are not challenged during the game.

If we were to see football players as representing citizens of a political state and the umpires and referees as representing the government of that state, we find that authority is seen as legitimate and necessary. In order for society to survive, so the analogy goes, we need rules and regulations and people to enforce them. The referees are like police: they enforce the rules and regulations, but they do not make them. And we, like the football players, obey these rules (laws), though we reserve the right to change them via our political process.

So football posits the good citizen who accepts the legitimacy of the government, though it also demonstrates that the representatives of the government, the referees, can make bad calls. In theory, the bad calls of the referees and umpires will also even out and benefit no one team. (There are mechanisms in football for protesting decisions, but the outcomes of games are never reversed, even if it can be proved that a call that might have cost a team the game was erroneous.) All that we ask of the umpires and referees is that they are impartial and interpret the rules and regulations of the game as honestly as they can.

"The Bomb" or Devastation through the Air

It is the forward pass that brought a new measure of excitement to the game, and of all kinds of forward passes, it is the long forward pass, the *bomb*, which is most thrilling. Football is a game involving conquering territory, and the bomb is the most dangerous and remarkable way of doing this. Of course the bomb is a low-percentage play, and all teams plan against it. But when it works, when the quarterback throws the ball forty or fifty yards and it is caught, there is a thrill that all the fans of the team feel. A daring enterprise has been successful.

The play itself is quite dramatic. There is that long, looping pass and, when the pass is caught, a sense of devastation on the part of the defending team. Often teams throw a bomb to loosen up the defense against the rush and don't necessarily expect the pass to be completed. The bomb is thrown for strategic reasons in such cases. But in other cases, when a team wants to make a big gain and throws a bomb, it is a great achievement.

The bomb also televises well and it is usually shown from a number of different angles so viewers will better be able to savor it. Sports reports on the television news often show the bomb as well, since it is a powerful visual, which means that a good bomb lives on long after the play itself has been completed. After a bomb there is also the wonderful pageant as the members of the offensive team trot down the field and take possession of a huge hunk of territory.

Of all bombs, the best one is that which results in a touchdown, for then fans need not worry about a fumble or an intercepted pass, which nullifies the splendor and impact of the bomb and leads to a depression in that a wonderful opportunity has been missed.

As in warfare, from which the term comes, the bomb then is an attempt to devastate an opponent, to achieve, through an extreme measure, some kind of important gain that will lead to victory. Quarterbacks are often evaluated in terms of their ability to throw the bomb and their success in doing so. (One quarterback, who played for the Oakland Raiders, was even called "the mad bomber," because of his propensity for throwing bombs.)

The Hail Mary, or Religion and Desperation

There is a special bomb, known as the *Hail Mary*, which is thrown in desperation at the end of a game. The defending team knows that the quarterback will be throwing a bomb into the end zone and defends against this by having a number of backs defend against the play. The quarterback throws the ball and hopes that somehow his receiver will be able to catch the ball, one way or another.

The fact that we call this particular kind of long bomb a Hail Mary makes overt the connection in the American mind between situations that we might describe as "desperate" (such as being a few points behind in a game and having only twenty or thirty seconds left) and religion. In times of crisis, football players and fans (as well as soldiers on the battlefield) call on some form of divine authority for inspiration and help. (Curiously enough, the players and fans of the opposing team may be calling on this same divine authority, which means that God will satisfy the prayers of at least half the players and fans.)

The Hail Mary is an attempt to generate divine intervention and produce, upon demand, so it would seem, a miracle. And there are just enough Hail Mary desperation passes that are caught to make them worth trying. Besides, when there is seemingly nothing else that a team can do, why not try a Hail Mary? Unfortunately, for most teams that attempt them, the game ends—to paraphrase T.S. Eliot—not with a bomb but a whimper.

Conversions

It is curious that we call kicking the point after a touchdown a *conversion*, for that term has a religious connotation that seems out of place. The conversion in football is a relatively mechanical process, and quality kickers can go through many seasons without missing one. Still, every once in a while a point after conversion is missed, and sometimes this lost point has an important outcome and leads to the loss of the game.

The "conversion" in religion involves changing from one religion to another, becoming a "convert." A conversion is usually some kind of a ritual activity associated with the changing of religions. In football it means taking advantage of an opportunity that one is given as the result of scoring a touchdown. A conversion represents, then, an act in which a point is "converted" from potentiality to actuality.

Of all conversions, the best one by far is after the successful Hail Mary touchdown pass. At moments such as these, unbelievers are converted to believers in mass, though, at the same time, the fans of the team that allowed the Hail Mary lose faith in a benevolent deity and one which, they had believed, favored their team.

The Interception or Shock and Demoralization

Of all the plays that shock and demoralize a team, the interception is preeminent. Blocking punts is generally more damaging, and recovering fumbles is always exciting, but the interception—because of the psychological importance of the forward pass, tied to its aesthetic beauty—is the most devastating kind of turnover. Blocking a punt often leads to a score (especially if the punter was deep in his own territory, near the goal line). But the team was about to turn the ball over anyway, so it does not have the kind of impact that the interception has, in which gallant plans are turned to naught and the team on offense suddenly finds itself on defense.

The interception is a signifier of something wrong with the offense. The quarterback may overthrow his receiver, or not notice a defensive back, or the receiver may run his route incorrectly. Whatever the reason, the intercepted forward pass represents the sudden snuffing out of offensive momentum and the sense of possibility that always rises when a team starts moving. If the forward pass is the ultimate offensive weapon in football, the interception is the ultimate defensive weapon, which brings instant (though generally momentary) demoralization and disequilibrium.

What football players and fans must learn to do is desensitize themselves so that the shock of the interception is minimalized and they can continue playing. Players cannot allow themselves to be overwhelmed by interceptions, nor must they pay little heed to them. Fortunately, after interceptions, both teams change their players around, so the unit that comes on to play defense is not implicated in the disaster. The defensive team's job is containment and damage control, and psychoanalytic studies have shown that players on defensive teams have different mind-sets than players on offensive teams.

Psychology plays an important role in football, and ''psyched up'' teams play more intensely and effectively than teams that become, for one reason or another, unnerved and ''down.'' Thus, learning how to deal with interceptions is of the utmost importance. Teams must learn how to cope with interceptions and not allow themselves to become deflated and psychologically devastated by them. In some cases, an interception is the crucial play in a game and preserves a win or makes possible a win when all seemed lost.

And that is why tens of thousands of people in a stadium let out an involuntary gasp of despair (while others scream with delight) when there is an interception, and the emotions of players flip-flop violently.

The Long Run or the Possibilities for Heroism

Next to the bomb, in my opinion, the long run is the most exciting and significant play in football. For it is with this play that our sense of escape from containment and of the possibility of individual heroism is most evident. The runners who break tackles, evade other players, cut and weave their way through defensive players, and accelerate at the right moment, are giving virtuoso displays of athletic ability.

There are some long runs that are not terribly interesting. A back may find an opening in the line and no defenders near him and race seventy yards for a touchdown. Of course we must admire his speed and perhaps the remarkable acceleration he displays as he races beyond the secondary, but this kind of a run is too simple and a rather flat kind of event. It lacks the element of conflict, in which the runner evades defending players and as the result of his skills makes a gain that another runner might not have been able to make.

This kind of a run shows the natural ability of the runner, who evades defenders and escapes from pursuers. What better metaphor for the hopes we all harbor as we confront the confining aspects of the world of work and the limitations of everyday existence—a chance for the demonstration of our heroic natures, of our abilities—a chance for heroism, for a moment of glory. And if we cannot approximate the long runs in our lives, we can gain some psychological benefit from watching the long runs of others.

For some people, the long run is the great event of their lives and one which they remember and savor. In football, as in life, the long run is a rare event. The game is such that when teams are evenly matched, long runs are quite rare. But there is always the possibility of the long run and the hope for it lurking in the minds of the players and of the fans.

Rivalries or the Importance of Tradition and History

Football has been played for more than one hundred years in American colleges and universities, so there are some rivalries that have lasted for decades and decades. This means that a given game between two teams that have been tradtional rivals is not just a game, but part of a continual relationship that may have lasted for fifty or seventy-five years. And the game takes on added significance because of this. The outcome of the game will effect the number of games won and lost between the two teams, so the game calls forth all kinds of latent and generally controlled feelings and animosities.

Football, then, weaves itself into American history and becomes intimately connected with rivalries between schools and regions—and perhaps even ideologies. (I am thinking here of the games that used to be played between Notre Dame, representing the Catholic Church and Catholic power in America, and Michigan State, representing the power of the state and of secular philosophy. These meetings were often exciting and were seen by many as being played for a mythical national championship.)

When we watch football and talk about it, we always do so against an historical frame of reference. We talk about great games, great players, and great teams of the near and distant past. Ironically, therefore, for a culture that is supposedly in danger of losing its historical memory, football is both a game played in the present and one that is firmly rooted in the past.

The rivalries in football remind us, also, that while we are a single nation, we have numerous regional differences—that are often shown in the style of football played in a particular region or conference. Writers and scholars have in fact suggested that there are a number of different Americas, ranging from the East coast, the Midwest, the South, the Pacific coast, and so on. These various Americas all have certain things in common but they are all quite different, too, in terms of their accents, food preferences, political views—and, often, their style of football.

One of the oldest rivalries involves the Big Ten teams of the Midwest with the Pacific Coast conference. The winningest teams from each conference play each other in the Rose Bowl in one of the most prestigious, if not the most prestigious, bowl game. In recent years the Pacific Coast conference has defeated the teams from the Big Ten a number of times, though the teams from the Big Ten were often favored. The styles of the two conferences are considerably different: whereas the Pacific Coast conference teams are known for speed, the forward pass, and a wide-open style, the Big Ten conference is famous for its size, the run, and a conservative style. I don't think it is too much of a generalization to suggest that the different styles of the two conferences represents the different styles of the two regions, though the Big Ten is now adopting the style of play of the Pacific coast conference teams.

Rankings or the Importance of Status

Football is a game that is violent and frenetic, but also mired in a sea of statistics. Before the football season begins, ranking are found in all the sports pages from the wire services and from various experts and gamblers, etc., who list (in an admittedly highly speculative enterprise) the top ten or twenty teams in the country. These lists are based on such criteria as past performances of the teams, their players and their coaches. Frequently the lists differ in assigning the top spots to the teams, though often there is surprising agreement.

Then, as the season progresses and there are upsets or poor performances from highly rated teams, the rankings change. The status a team has plays an important role in recruiting new players, so the matter really is important. High school stars consider such matters as whether they will be on an important team, whether they will be able to play, and whether they will get national television coverage when they decide what school to attend, since these factors often help determine whether they will be able to move on to play professional football.

America is, in terms of its official political philosophy, an egalitarian country. This is part of our heritage. We do not have a heritage of royalty and we believe that all people are created equal. In egalitarian countries, curiously, there is enormous competition and a desire to distinguish oneself from others and a great deal of pressure to climb to the top of whatever "mountain" one is interested in. Thus, we are passionately concerned with who is winning and losing rather than how well a game is being played and with which team can lay claim to the mythical national championship—in collegiate football, that is. In professional football we have the Superbowl which settles the question.

This passion for ranking teams might suggest that there is something inherent in people for categorizing people and groups (like us, not like us) and ranking entities (high, low) according to some scale of values. In egalitarian countries, prestige is not conferred by birth (by ascription, as the sociologists put it) but by attainments (by achievement, as the sociologists put it). In principle, people who are willing to work hard enough can attain success (whatever that might be) since, and here football and other sports are ritually invoked, "the playing field is level."

In truth, we know that once families attain a certain level of wealth and power, their children will have better life chances than other children born into poorer families, which means that middle- and upper-class families are able to give their children advantages that help preserve the social inequalities that exist in American culture. But the myth of our being a classless, essentially all middle-class society dominates—aided by the myth of "shirtsleeves to shirtsleeves in three generations," which suggests that eventually the children of the wealthy become spoiled wastrels and that in a few generations they or their children are back in the working classes.

It is curious, if you think about it, how big a role rankings play in a society that is based on egalitarian ideals.

Stars and the Existence of Hierarchy

In every decent football team we find stars—players who have an important impact on the game, who pose a threat to the opposing team and who attract a great deal of media attention. It is impossible to focus our attention on an entire team, so these stars serve as useful points of reference for the fans. In the Hollywood entertainment world, stars are, we are often told, "made" and not born. Press agentry and all kinds of other things are factors. In football, on the other hand, stars must perform. Stardom is based on achievement.

The fact that we have stars raises an interesting question. How do you reconcile hierarchies (stars and ordinary players) and equality? The answer is that we have equality of opportunity, which means that everyone has the chance to be a star but not everyone has the talent to be one. So we have the best of both worlds—an egalitarian society that has stars in various fields.

In some cases stars fade. In the competitive world of football, a star one year finds himself eclipsed by a bigger star who joins the team. Or the star has a bad year. And some players, who look like they will be stars, never achieve stardom. They start as quarterback or halfback or whatever position and don't do well, and are replaced by a second-stringer who suddenly shows himself to be a star.

This raises an interesting point. Why is it that coaches and sports-writers and everyone else miss so many stars? How is it that a star can spend so much time on the sidelines and never get a chance? (We can ask this about other fields, such as opera and orchestra conducting.) There is something about people who manage to become seen as stars that distracts us from others who may be more talented but who never get the opportunity they deserve.

In college football, the high schools serve as feeder systems for the colleges, and high school players who have achieved stardom generally manage to carry this over to the colleges. This stardom is usually based on their records and on their physical abilities. But in the crucible that is college football, stars fade and others start burning brightly.

In the mid-eighties, I taught at the University of Southern California for a year as a visiting professor. In the school newspaper that fall there was an article about a highly regarded freshman who had been snared by USC. He said that he thought his biggest problem would be dealing with the press. That is, he felt assured of his stardom, and the only question in his mind was how to handle his forthcoming stardom. Unfortunately, things didn't quite work out the way he thought they would and he ended up as a rather ordinary player who either never achieved his potential or didn't have that much potential and only discovered it when he got to USC.

Football is a team sport, and even if a player has star quality, if he doesn't have a good team to support him, he will never be able to do much. So stardom involves being a member of a team that will allow one's talents to be realized. The star is dependent on his team and, ironically, it is all the other players that make stardom possible. The best of all situations is to be on a team full of stars in which each facilitates the stardom of the others.

The term *star* has now been eclipsed by the term *superstar*. It seems to relegate stardom to a kind of ordinariness by linguistic inflation. Once there were stars and ordinary players; now there are superstars, and many players who we once considered ordinary are now stars. And what of us, the ordinary people, who gaze upon these superstars? Does the existence of superstars make the lives of ordinary people seem insignificant and petty?

Team Records or the Importance of Bureaucracy

Football, like all sports, swims in a sea of statistics. As we watch a game, we are constantly informed about this or that record being broken, about how many games the teams have played with one another over the years, and which team has won how may games, etc. We have a curious alliance between a sport based on chance, error, physical abilities, and violence and the bureaucratic record-keeping mentality which takes note of everything and enters it into some database for use at some time.

One reason records are so important is that in American society, we are obsessed with achievement since it is the only way to attain distinction (unlike in aristocratic societies, where birth and breeding do this for you). In elitist, aristocratic societies, it is *who you are* (which means who your parents are) that is crucial; in egalitarian societies, it is *what you do*.

These records also play an important part in negotiations about salaries in professional football, which is, we must remember, a business that exists to make a profit. Outstanding college players can offer statistics which they use to obtain huge salaries and bonuses for signing with a given professional team.

So we have an interesting union of physical capacity and team effort with record-keeping and bureaucracy. Football is a game played by athletes and run by agents, accountants, and lawyers.

The Fans or Community for the Moment

It is not unusual to have 70,000 people attend a game, which is something we must keep in mind. For the game is played before huge numbers of highly partisan fans, who root for one team or another (especially in college games) and who identify strongly with a particular team.

America is a country of immigrants, a country made up of all kinds of different racial, ethnic, linguistic, and religious groups. Unlike some countries, which are unified in many of these aspects (Japan is almost 100 percent Japanese, in terms of ethnic stock, for instance and Italy is more than 90 percent Catholic, in terms of religious belief) America is diverse in every aspect.

What unifies America? One thing is our popular culture—our television programs, our movies, and our sports—which reflect our basic values and which, in subtle ways, "indoctrinate" people into this value system.

In many cases, we find temporary alliances in American society. This is what happens in a football game. People who differ in many ways come together, momentarily, to root for their team and form a momentary community. One of the theories used to explain American democracy holds that Americans belong to so many different voluntary associations and groups (such as clubs, religions and political organizations) that their allegiances are divided and you don't get the kind of ideological intensity found in other countries, where political and religious beliefs are much more focused.

We might say that the existence of football fans precludes the development of fanaticisms, of the left or right, in religious belief and politics. The crowd at the football game experiences a form of momentary community, a sense of oneness that provides important psychological support and has political implications.

Marxists make a different argument. They argue that the spectacle in football is diversionary and distracts people from serious consideration of social and political problems. It is the old "bread and circuses" argument. Keep the mind of the people off serious matters by keeping them constantly entertained with matters of no real consequence. Instead of people focusing their emotions on their real-life situation, and perhaps doing something about it, they invest their emotions in games.

These games provide a catharsis, a way people can deal with the powerful emotions raging within them (caused, the Marxists would argue, by the inequalities in society and the exploitation the masses suffer at the hands of the capitalists). This means that football, though it is just a sport, inadvertently plays an important role in American society and has political significance. The more time we spend and emotional energy we invest in the games, the less time we have for serious political activity.

This argument is, I think, a bit simple-minded, for though statistics show that we have a relatively low percentage of people voting in national elections, this figure could mean that the American public is satisfied with things, in general. Also, Americans vote in all kinds of elections, seemingly all the time, so it is somewhat incorrect to argue that Americans have little political concern or consciousness.

The huge crowds at football games make one think of the giant crowds mustered by the Germans and various communist regimes for political ceremonials. Crowds do have a power to carry people along, as if by contagion, and political leaders, using pageantry and other means, can generate incredible emotional responses in people. But the crowds at stadiums are people who have come voluntarily and who have paid for the privilege of being at the game, too. They are separated by team loyalties (and other loyalties), and their emotions are tied to competing teams playing a game that has, one might argue, democratic implications.

The football stadium might be described as a kind of *sacred space* in American society—a privileged place where rituals of great significance (the games) are performed. Some philosophers distinguish between *sacred space* (where culturally important things occur) and *profane space* (where nothing particularly significant takes place). You sense some kind of a different quality in sacred space. The lighting, the color, the grandeur, the spectacle—all suggest that one is somehow closer to the gods or to some kind of qualitatively different kind of experience.

Fans would not recognize that the stadiums are sacred, of course, but they do know that they have powerful emotional experiences at the games (there are often tears of joy or sorrow, there is heartache at "tragic" losses or feelings of incredible exultation), which suggests a camouflaged religious experience. The game of football is highly structured and ritualistic, and where there is ritual there is some kind of a religious experience.

The Football Widows or Sexual Differentiation in Fans

During the football season, millions of women become *football widows*, women who seemingly have "lost" their husbands to the game of football. There are so many games shown on television on weekends (and there is Monday night football, and often football is shown on other weekday evenings) that you can spend incredible amounts of time watching the sport.

The term *football widow* suggests that watching televised football is essentially a masculine activity, and the television commercials for beer, trucks, tires, cars, and other products traditionally purchased by men suggests that advertisers believe this is the case. We see that the stadiums are full of men and women, but women, as the term football widow suggests, don't watch football on television—at least to the extent that men do. Why is it that women go to football games but don't watch it on television?

What the term suggests is that televised football has the power to "kill" a relationship, if only for a temporary period of time, between husbands and wives. The football widow regains her husband, so one imagines, after the bowl games and the Superbowl, which means her widowhood lasts approximately five months.

Women, so the theory goes, might enjoy the experience of going to a game and perhaps rooting for their college team (or city's professional team), but they may be put off by the violence in the game and might not appreciate its many subtleties. I find this hard to believe. I think the differentiation is caused by the socialization process, women don't play tag football when they are young and, in the past, have more or less been excluded from the game. It is traditionally played by men.

Now that more and more women go to college, however, and attend the games, it is likely that things have changed and women understand and appreciate the game. If they don't watch as much television football as men it is because, quite often, they have other obligations which take up their time, since even women who work end up, so statistics show, doing most of the cooking and housework.

The football widow, then, is the victim of a system which penalizes women, in part because they acquiesce and accept the status quo. When women become more assertive (which they might have learned had they played football when growing up) and make men do an equal amount of work in the house, their status will change.

Padding or Hypermasculinity and Feminization

Football is a contact sport and one in which there are numerous injuries. To minimize injuries, the players wear protective padding. (Curiously enough, rugby is also a contact sport, but players don't wear any padding.) What significance does this padding have? Consider the huge shoulder pads that the players wear. These shoulder pads exaggerate their shoulders and minimize their waists, generating an effect that has been termed *hypermasculine*.

According to Alan Dundes, a folklorist at the University of California in Berkeley, there is a great deal of hidden sexual content in football, which accounts (in part) for its popularity. As he points out, the football has "ends" (unlike a basketball or a volleyball); certain players are called ends, and the most important part of the game involves penetrating the opponent's "end zones."

From a psychoanalytic point of view, the game involves two teams that are attempting to dominate one another sexually, which means one team is trying to assert its masculinity (by penetrating the opponent's end zones the most frequently) and, in so doing, feminize the other team. Of course all of this is subliminal. The players are not aware of the psychosexual significance of their activities. The same applies to the fans. But underneath it all, so the theory goes, there is a kind of subliminal understanding of what is at stake.

And that is why players and fans become so emotionally involved in the games and why you hear such groans or such elation at times. This feminization is, of course, only relative, but it still is devastating. That is why players are often so demonstrative after scoring touchdowns, and either wave the ball for all to see or spike it (or do both). This is rubbing salt into the wounds and emphasizing the extent of the triumph.

There are also interesting homosexual implications to certain aspects of the game. For example, the quarterback stands, bending over the center, in a position that is very suggestive. And players often hug one another and pat one another on the rear end. Because the players have become hypermasculine, due to their padding and uniforms, this behavior is not considered suspect in any way. The public nature of the game hides the significance of these acts for most people. In addition, there are elements of male bonding that are seen as quite normal in the context of an athletic competition.

Two different groups of people find Dundes' theories particularly interesting. The homosexual groups, who say "see, everyone does it" and feminist groups who say, "see how feminization is equated with losing and seen as somehow negative." One thing that occurs to me as I think about shoulder pads and the whole hypermasculine look of football is that this look has moved into women's fashions.

Was this look in some way connected to a desire, on the part of women, to partake of the psychological consequences and benefits of hypermasculinity and an unconscious attempt by women to masculinize themselves? In attempting to escape from images of docile femininity, did women (at least those who wore the big shoulders) masculinize themselves? Did this fashion represent an attempt by women to de-emphasize their sexual characteristics and move to a less defined gender status?

Pom-Pom Girls and Cheerleaders

The women cheerleaders and pom-pom girls show what role women are expected to play at the games (and in American society): they are on the sidelines, watching the men play. They may encourage them on, and jump up and down to get the fans to cheer, but the role of the cheerleaders and pom-pom girls is of secondary importance. The game itself is what is significant and they are simply spectators.

In this respect, football is somewhat dated, for women have no serious role to play. (Women don't play any role in baseball, either, but baseball doesn't have cheerleaders.) They are basically sexual objects. This is most evident in some professional teams that have a corps of beautiful women with generally scanty uniforms who do various steps, in unison, much like chorus girls. One gets the best of both worlds: heroic super-males, battling like gladiators on the field and beautiful women, doing mechanized bumps and grinds, on the sidelines.

This linkage of feminized sexual display and male heroism is not accidental. These women (or their various counterparts) can be seen as the "rewards" the heroes can expect after their ordeals and triumphs. Heroes traditionally undertake great adventures, undergo various ordeals, and after their triumphs get to marry the princess or some other desirable woman. These women, then, serve two functions: they delight the male (and perhaps female) spectators, and they serve as subtle reminders of the rewards players can claim after they have triumphed on the field.

If the players have been feminized by defeat, sexual activity takes on a different dimension, and becomes a kind of consolation prize for men whose male identities have been (temporarily) weakened. It also becomes an incentive to try harder next week so they can have the kind of sex heroes have—which, we may presume, is the best kind.

Bowed Heads of the Losers

At certain points in games which are tightly contested, or games in which teams are defeated by underdogs, we often see shots of players on the losing team sitting on the sidelines with their heads bowed. Some are in tears. Some hang towels over their heads. Some sit with their hands over their heads, unable to watch the game.

All of these behaviors signify defeat and humiliation. In some contests, the game isn't decided until the last moment and then, when it is, players on the losing team are shocked. In other games, a team experiences a long, humiliating ordeal, and its self-image suddenly seems terribly wrong.

Since players derive a great deal of psychological support from being on a winning team or a great team, the impact is particularly strong. Especially with young college players, whose identities are often tied to their teams. What we see is a kind of battlefield shock, as the spectre of defeat and the psychological devastation that comes with it grows stronger and stronger. One of the important things that happens to students in colleges and universities is that they must learn to face the reality of their limitations and experience failure in ways that will not be destructive.

Many students who dream of being doctors or lawyers suddenly find that they cannot pass introductory physics or organic chemistry, and that they must find new careers for themselves. (One-third of my freshman class was premed, and I would imagine this still holds true in many of our better universities.) And players who dream of being stars or derive psychological benefit from being on great teams suddenly have to face the reality of losses—of games and of self-images.

Fortunately for them, football is only a game and is of relatively minor importance, if you think about it. (It has been said that people identify with political organizations and religious cults, for example, to shield themselves from the fact that their lives are "only minor events in the ongoing universe.") Of course, to a person involved in a game, it is the score and the events on the field that are all important, but it is all a matter of the moment. In football, fortunately, there is always next week.

Even professional players, who are much more mature and for whom the game is both a sport to be enjoyed and a way of earning a living, get emotionally involved in games. Football games are often exciting and everyone involved, players and fans, become caught up in the action. It is the nature of the game that they are frequently decided in the very last minutes or seconds which means there is an emotional buildup and great excitement is generated. For the losers, after some crucial play, there is a feeling of heartbreak and despair, and the world is turned upside down.

The defeat, however, is only seen as a temporary setback, for there is always next week's game. The fact that this is so has important implications for our political system, for in democracies, defeat is also seen as a temporary setback, The contending parties accept the democratic political system and do not try to subvert it since being defeated does not mean one's political fortunes (and party) will be annihilated whereas in the ancient Roman combats games were perilous. A gladiator who lost was often put to death.

It is ironic that in American politics, parties that win overwhelmingly in presidential elections often come to grief. The last three American presidents who won overwhelming victories—Lyndon Johnson, Richard Nixon, and Ronald Reagan—ended up having their presidencies tarnished, and in the case of Nixon being forced out of office. A president who wins too easily tends to fall victim to an exaggerated sense of his importance and power, just as teams that win overwhelming victories often become overconfident.

What I am discussing here is our essentially egalitarian and democratic attitudes and values which inform our politics and are, to a degree, reflected in and reinforced by the game of football, and by many of our other sports and entertainments.

This also explains why we tend to root for the underdog. We want the underdog to win since we want to make our society as egalitarian as we can. We recognize the existence of inequalities (in teams as well as in socio-economic life), but we always try to diminish the significance of these differences. And we identify with the underdog team. When an underdog team beats its opponent and there is an "upset," we feel that this is a kind of vindication of our political order, and the triumph mirrors the triumphs that we hope to achieve in our personal lives.

Football on Television: The Mediated Experience

When we watch football on television, as millions of us do on Saturdays, Sundays, Monday evenings and, occasionally at other times, we are having a different experience from people who are at the game. They are seeing the game from a unique perspective, though many stadiums have introduced gigantic television screens which enable those at the games to see the game as it is mediated through the television cameras.

Televised football teaches us that there are many different ways of seeing the same thing, that no one perspective is privileged. Few of us pay any attention to the camera work at games or even notice the number of cameras and cameramen and other technicians who are needed to televise the game. It is not unusual to use five or six cameras in televising a game (in Superbowls they often use twice that number) which means the director is constantly choosing between any number of different kinds of shots at any given moment.

There is a great deal of quick-cutting between endzone shots, side-line shots, longshots and close-ups, action shots and girlie shots (shots of attractive women spectators) and numerous replays, in which a given play is shown over again from several different perspectives. It is this remarkable camera work that has led some media theorists to suggest that football is the best thing (from a purely technical point of view) shown on television and that a football game is very close, in many respects, to an avant-garde film or video (in which we see the same sophisticated technical effects).

The camera work on television also implies democratic values since everything that happens is seen from many different perspectives. This camera work is anti-absolutist and, in essence, pluralist, just like American society and the American political order. There is no one true view of a play, and sometimes a different camera shot reveals things that were not seen from some other position or perspective (such as the one you may think is the correct one).

The Four Political Cultures Found in Complex Societies

Let us return to Wildavsky's thesis that we always find four political cultures in democratic societies. There are basic values and beliefs relating to rules and prescriptions and the strength of group boundaries that produce these groupings: competitive individualists, egalitarians, hierarchical collectivists, and fatalists. The egalitarians tend to criticize hierarchical and elitist aspects of the political and social order and seek to minimize all differences between people. These groups all need one another and constantly battle with one another for dominance.

If people were perfectly logical and followed the implications of their political culture (assuming Wildavsky is correct, that is) we would find football watched primarily by hierarchical collectivists, for the game seems to be most closely connected with this set of beliefs. (Boxing, tennis, or fencing would be sports for competitive individualists, in that these activities do not involve teamwork and reliance on others for success.) There are hierarchies in football, with its stars and its ordinary people, with the backfield players having great status and the line (the so-called grunts) having less. There are superior figures, the coaches, who teach the players and more or less control them. They also guide them and look after them, and the players recognize that their success is tied to the group of which they are a member.

Thus many of the phenomena found in hierarchical collectivist political cultures are found in the sport. There is also the tendency, mentioned earlier, of Americans to root for the underdogs, which suggests that there may be various mixtures of these four political cultures in us, though, according to the theory, we all identify with one or another of these groups. Fatalists would not find the game terribly satisfying since it is a contest and there are upsets, and individualists would find the team elements somewhat troubling, though they might identify with the stars who play brilliantly (in spite of their teams, in some cases).

Football is a metaphor for life and politics in America. Football teaches us, indirectly and without calling attention to the fact, that it has a significance beyond itself. It is nearly a uniquely American sport which plays an important role in our society and culture and speaks to us in more profound ways than we might imagine.

Last Thursday night the President attempted to persuade the nation that his decision to deal arms to Iran was merely a gesture of rapprochement, but logic suggests that those arms were meant to secure the release of U.S. hostages in Lebanon. What shocks Americans about this transaction is that it seems so uncharacteristic of a President who has railed against trading with terrorists, and who appears to sense that his public agrees with his position. In fact, the effort to free individuals in Lebanon at a possible extreme cost is perfectly consistent with the way Reagan has always conducted the presidency's business. In forests of complex issues, Reagan likes to point to the trees, to individuals. The suggestion is that individuals embody policies, that if one appreciates the situation or nature of a particular person, he will also understand general actions taken in that person's behalf.

—Roger Rosenblatt, Time, *Nov. 24, 1986*

3

The Iran-Contra Hearings: A Case-Study in Political Theatre

On Political Theatre

What is it about the Iran-Contra hearings that makes it possible to describe them as "political theatre?" Why did these hearings grab the attention of the American public with such tenacity and hold it for such a long time? And what does the term "political theatre" mean?

Political theatre, as I use the term, involves any matters concerning the role of government that have, for one reason or another, a dramatic quality—and that also have a public character. In order to have theatre you have to have an audience, but you also have to have actors and actresses who captivate the public. Political theatre doesn't necessarily involve battles between parties or other adversaries; thus when the Tower Committee held a press conference and announced its findings, that was political theatre. The event was dramatic because the public would learn, for the first time, what the committee discovered.

But this event was mild compared to the joint Senate and House hearings that are popularly known as the Iran-Contra Hearings. In these hearings, carried on radio and television, we found the elements that provide classic political theatre: a remarkable cast of characters recounting incredible tales of their doings, all of which involved the foreign policy of the United States of America and, not incidentally, huge sums of money.

The Senate and House decided on a novel joint-hearings approach in order to avoid overlapping and to expedite the hearings. There were two different committees—one from the Senate and one from the

House of Representatives—but they met and carried out the hearings jointly. Both parties faced problems with the hearings. The Republicans couldn't be too defensive or ideological and couldn't seem to be trying to cover things up. And the Democrats couldn't seem too bloodthirsty or partisan and couldn't seem to want to destroy the president. On the other hand, both parties wanted to use the hearings for their own purposes while seeming not to do so.

The Setting

The setting is an important part of theatre: it provides the audience with a context, with numerous indicators of what the actors may be like and how to regard the events that are to transpire. The most important setting for the hearings was the Senate Hearing Room, a huge chamber that had been the site of many other historic hearings. There was a gigantic flag against the wall and there were banks of desks, rising from the floor of the chamber up to a considerable height. Along these banks of desks sat the Senators and Congressmen, the aides and the lawyers who had been employed by the two committees.

Those who testified were on the floor behind a large table (frequently with their counsel), and they looked up at the various members of the joint-committees. Slightly in front of the people who testified were photographers and camera operators. The ambience was formal and the spatiality of the setting monumental; that and the many important congressional leaders from both parties generated the sense that something of great consequence was taking place. In addition, of course, there was the matter at hand, which involved American foreign policy, and in particular our shipping arms to the Iranians in an attempt to buy the freedom of Americans who had been kidnapped by terrorists linked in various ways to the Iranian government and cause.

The hearings were marked by the traditional politeness and civility that characterize relations in the Congress. This decorum dominated the hearings, though at times the lawyers breached it.

The Cast of Characters

The hearings presented to the American public a really remarkable cast of characters, ranging from a retired Army general long associated with right-wing, ultraconservative causes to a beautiful secretary, who assisted her boss, Lieutenant Colonel Oliver North, in shredding documents. There was also a somewhat duplicitous Iranian businessman who had become an American citizen and who was involved with the goings-on strictly to make money, a Contra leader, various former CIA operatives, Lieutenant Col. North, as well as the Secretary of State and the Secretary of Defense.

Some of the people testified for relatively short periods of time and others, like North, were on for a week and had an incredible amount of national exposure.

The *Rashomon* Phenomenon

Rashomon is a classic Japanese film about a man and his beautiful wife who meet a famous bandit. The bandit overpowers the husband, ties him up and rapes his wife. After the rape, the husband is killed. That much is certain. But how he was killed and the events that transpired are somewhat confusing, for each of the characters tells a different story of what happened at the trial of the bandit. This includes the dead husband, whose story is told by a shaman in a trance. There is also a woodcutter, who came upon the scene after the rape, who tells a story that is different from all the other stories. So we have many different first hand accounts of the same event, which I call the *Rashomon* phenomenon.

The same thing happened at the hearings. Many of the people testifying agreed with one another about certain parts of their stories but contradicted one another about other parts of their stories. The more people testified, the more confusing things became and the committee (and the audience) had the task of figuring out who was telling the truth and who was lying, and which parts of the testimony were true and which parts seemed to be false. It was all confusing and incredibly fascinating.

Hearing the Story

The whole story was told by the characters. It was something like an epistolary novel in which we follow action only as it is recounted in letters by the protagonists. The term *hearings* is apt, for what we heard and saw were people sitting in chairs asking and answering questions. You wouldn't think that this could be very exciting, but in fact it was.

This is because the tales recounted were so fantastic and the secrets that the joint committees were trying to get at so important, that millions of people followed the hearings with fascination and shock.

The film *My Dinner with Andre* showed that you don't need action if you have great conversation. In this film two friends have dinner and the conversation is so fabulous, the tales so incredible, that audiences were mesmerized. We are back, here, to the old tradition of the tale-teller, who entertained people with recounting the actions of heroic figures.

Actually, there were two *stories* in the hearings. The first was the story of what happened—of what people did. That, in turn, was the basis for the second story, which evolved in real time as people watched and which had a dramatic impact on the American political order. This second story involved the press and various political and governmental figures and the politics of the day. In a sense, the story was evolving as people learned more about what had happened in the past, for as things came to light, the reputation and power of the president were profoundly affected.

Talking Heads

The hearings were on for a long time and many people watched them. Some people became "hooked" on the hearings and watched them continually, while others sampled them. What is so remarkable about the hearings, as a television genre, is that they were comprised of nothing but *talking heads*, to use the language of people in the television business. In television, which is a visual medium, the conventional wisdom is that talking heads are boring, and programs that show people just talking are to be avoided.

Thus, television news continually looks for pictorially interesting stories, ones that have strong visual appeal, even if it has to neglect stories that may be more important but that only involve a talking head.

How do we explain the power of these hearings? Why did they fascinate (perhaps mesmerize is a better word) so many people? One answer is that the conventional wisdom about talking heads is wrong and that if talking heads have interesting things to say, people will watch. Television may be a visual medium, but it is also an auditory one, a fact which tends to be overlooked. (It is only recently that television sets started being produced with good quality audio speakers, for example.)

The hearings were an attempt by the Congress to unravel a complicated ball of string (the actions of the various people who testified) and resembled most closely, I would suggest, a mystery story. The great innovation of the hearings was that they created a new kind of detective, one with multiple personalities, namely the entire joint committee. Those who listened to the hearings on the radio could not participate with the television viewers in one of the most important aspects of detection: noticing the way people respond to questions by scrutinizing their facial expressions and body language.

What did everyone want to know? The basic questions were what happened in the dealings with the Iranians, how was the money transferred to the Contras (and what happened to the money) and, finally, what did the president know?

The Absent Hero

Throughout all the hearings, one name kept coming up—Oliver North. He was the constant in the testimony, the figure around whom everything seemed to revolve. He seemed to have been everywhere at the same time, a kind of omnipresent force. The more the hearings progressed, the larger he loomed as a presence, though he was one who was only talked about, for he had not testified and for a while there seemed to be a question as to whether he would testify. The more the hearings progressed, the more his name came up. It was like a play in which the main character is continually the subject of conversation of minor characters. This makes the entrance of the main character into the action more exciting and dramatic.

The Absent Hero Moves Onstage

When North did finally testify, he gave a bravura performance. The joint committees seem to have underestimated him and the American public didn't know what to expect. He had been well coached by his lawyers and turned out to be a clean-cut, voluble, intelligent man who freely admitted to telling lies, shredding documents, and transferring ("diverting" was the term he used) funds the Iranians had paid for arms to the Contras, even though this almost certainly broke the law. He was a superb story teller and had an emotional quaver to his voice that was touching. He was also well mannered and polite, a quintessential, model American who also (as his medals showed) was a war hero. The committee found itself facing a yarn-spinning patriot, a combination soldier-secret agent who generated a strong but short-lived Ollie-mania in the American public.

He had been characterized in previous testimony as a "loose cannon" who seemed to be out of control. Yet he claimed that he was authorized to do everything he did, and that he had sent up numerous memos to his superiors detailing what he was doing. In certain areas his superiors didn't want to know precisely what he was doing because his activities were rather questionable. One thing was certain: for a lieutenant colonel he had incredible power, and the conclusion that most people reached was that this was because he was doing what other people, with great power, wanted him to do. Opinion polls reveal most Americans feel that President Reagan was lying when he said he didn't know what was going on in his own White House. They also reveal that most Americans don't feel North should be sent to prison for his acts and resent his being used as a fall guy.

Understanding North's Appeal

There are a number of reasons to explain North's appeal. He seems, in many ways, a typical or representative American: he is hard working, a man of action, a family man, a man with a sense of humor, a man dedicated to America. There is also a hint of zealotry in him, a kind of passionate intensity and single-mindedness that we find in many Americans. He is a man with whom people can easily identify.

On the other hand, he is also a James Bond kind of figure who led a life of adventure and intrigue, who associated with powerful figures from all over the world, who was sent on dangerous missions by some kind of an "M" figure, and was involved with events of great significance. Like Bond he was also "captured" by powerful and misguided figures (read the joint committee here) and forced to undergo ordeals— the hearings.

He also had a beautiful secretary, Fawn Hall, a former model, who injected the only element of sexuality into the meetings. And, in the Bond tradition, she was only of incidental significance, though unlike Bond, the relationship between North and Hall was, he asserted, perfectly correct since, as North put it, "there was no hanky-panky."

It is possible to list the differences between North's life and the ordinary American's life to show this James Bond aspect of North's life more clearly.

North	John Q. Public
Danger, excitement	Routine life
Knows world leaders	Knows ordinary people
Hyperactive	Active to neurasthenic
Heroic past	Ordinary past
Wants to save world	Wants to lead good life

This list may be a bit exaggerated, but it does point up the difference between North's activities and that of the typical American. North had an office in the White House, knew and worked with what might be called the power elite in Washington and elsewhere, and combined the attributes of the typical American with the James Bond spy in a somewhat Americanized version of this figure.

Americans could both identify with North (he seemed to be a regular guy who made a number of grammatical mistakes when he spoke) and see him as quite different and rather intriguing. Like Bond, there seems to be an oedipal attachment to an older father figure—in this case, Bill Casey, the head of the Central Intelligence Agency. And like all secret agents, there seems to be an element of paranoia in North's personality. Thus we find all the absurd and often humorous code-names and mania for secrecy that gave his testimony a sense of both drama and comedy.

The hearings raised the problem of how democracies control covert actions by intelligence agencies, a subject that was talked about a great deal, and the larger question of the relation between the Congress, the legislative branch of the government, and the presidency, the executive branch of government. American government is based on the separation of powers, and many congressmen felt that the Iran-Contra hearings were really about an attempt by the executive to evade congressional restrictions and laws and seize control of foreign policy in underhanded and devious ways. This explains why the committee,

despite numerous political and ideological differences in its membership, functioned so smoothly, for at the heart of things there was the
matter of defending congressional rights.

The Mitchell Speech: Fighting Fire with Fire

It took only a short while for the Democratic members of the
committee to realize that the way to deal with North was by "fighting
fire with fire." When they had asked him questions before, he had
frequently answered them by delivering long speeches defending his
actions and his principles. He seized the opportunity when given any
opening.

The new strategy was epitomized by Senator George Mitchell of
Maine, who used his time to "lecture" North by offering a long and
very moving speech, which countered North's ideas and gave a lesson
in civics to the American public. Mitchell had been a judge before he
became a senator, and he talked about swearing in new citizens—in
very emotional and moving terms. He made the point that America is a
pluralistic society and that all kinds of different people with different
beliefs live in America, and that people may love America and still
disagree with one another about politics among other things.

This was the approach that was used by the Democrats in the latter
part of the North hearings. He ended up listening to lectures by the
Democrats, though the Republicans gave him a chance to speak,
especially those who agreed with him about supporting the Contras.
The two committees were divided on the Contra issues—there were
some Democrats who supported giving aid to them and some Republicans who opposed giving them aid. It was not, by any means, a party
issue.

The Poindexter Testimony

It was the Poindexter testimony that was most crucial, for he was the
one who finally answered the question "what did the president
know?" Poindexter's answer was that the president did not know
about the diversion of funds, and that it was Poindexter's own decision
to keep the president uninformed. "The buck," Poindexter said,
"stopped with me." Despite this assertion, and countless statements

by President Reagan that he did not know what was going on, many Americans still believe that the president did know what was happening and has lied to the American public. It is just that nobody could find a smoking gun to prove this.

Poindexter's persona was of particular interest. His background was remarkable. In 1958 he graduated first in his class from Annapolis and was also chosen brigade commander, which meant that he was rated first in his leadership ability, as well. He then went on to get a Ph.D. in nuclear physics from the California Institute of Technology, one of the premier science institutions in the country.

But what did the American public see on the screen when they tuned in to watch the Poindexter testimony? A bland, mild-mannered, bald, pipe-smoking person who seemed to have the mentality of a petty bureaucrat and who, despite having something close to a photographic memory (or so it was alleged), remembered hardly anything. He was a colorless character who spoke in a soft, measured monotone and seemed to be devoid of charisma.

Was North what Poindexter once was, and was Poindexter what North would become? (North himself had bureaucratic tendencies and mentioned that he had kept careful records of all his activities, expenses, etc.) What was striking about the Poindexter testimony was that he was a man of obvious intelligence who seemed to have very little feeling for democratic processes. He took responsibility for the diversion of funds to support the Contras, assuming he could keep this decision secret and recognizing that it was a controversial and dangerous thing to do. Were these the actions of a quintessential military man? And if so, does his testimony raise questions about the extent to which our military leaders understand and are sympathetic with democratic processes? Is there a military mindset which is fundamentally at conflict with democratic processes? Lieutenant Colonel North claimed he was "authorized" to do everything he did and that he was, in essence, following orders. One of the questions raised by the hearings was when should a military man refuse to follow orders?

Poindexter ended up as the real fall guy, who assumed responsibility for the events that had transpired. In an article on Poindexter, *Time* Magazine suggested Poindexter had been appointed by Reagan since he thought he could control him easily, and that Poindexter was badly miscast since he was really a technician and had the temperament to be a superb support person. Whatever the case, it was the Poindexter testimony that was the most revealing. After his testimony, the hearings held little suspense and the public more or less lost interest.

The Importance of the Camera

The average person who watches a television program pays little attention to the camera work. It is almost assumed that programs just appear and that the various shots one sees are somehow "natural." Actually, it takes the expertise of numerous technicians and specialists to make a television program: there is lighting to be considered, there is sound, and there is camera work.

The typical television program uses a number of cameras, which are coordinated by a director, who tells each cameraperson what kind of a shot is desired. The visual look of a program, then, is created by the director, who orders various kinds of shots and chooses among them.

Audiences learn how to interpret or make sense of various shots, almost by osmosis. Thus, the long shots of the Senate Hearing Room established a sense of context and showed viewers all the "actors" participating in the hearings: the press, the lawyers, the guards, the senators and congressmen, the people testifying, the members of the audience and so on. On the other hand, when the camera zoomed in for a close-up of a person testifying or asking a question, the viewers could not help but feel that something important was going on and that they should take special notice.

The camera work is always done for a purpose and directs the attention of the viewers. "Look," it says, "this is important and you had better pay special attention," when it zooms in to an extreme close-up, in which we see only a face. "Look at the person's face for signs that might reveal something interesting." Or, when it switches to a long shot or establishing shot, it suggests we take a moment to get the big picture again.

The cameras in the Iran-Contra hearings were extremely active, shuttling back and forth between the lawyers for the committees and the people testifying, splitting the screen at times, showing profile against profile as if to suggest some kind of confrontation. There were many reaction shots, in which someone's response to a statement was flashed on the screen for the viewers to take note of and make sense of.

When people watch television, they learn to pay attention (and the shots used by the director make them pay special attention) to visual and nonverbal aspects of communcation—body language, facial expression, the clothes characters wear, the style of people's eyeglasses and anything else that functions as a sign and offers information.

The way the director cuts from shot to shot has an impact as well as the shots the director uses. Quick cutting, moving from shot to shot rapidly, conveys a sense of excitement and energizes viewers. The opposite kind of cutting, lingering over shots and having the camera move around without cutting very often, conveys a different sense.

A person listening to the hearings on radio would have a different sense of them from a person who watched them on television. The radio listener might have a better sense of the arguments made, since there is nothing visual to distract one from the words spoken, but the television viewer has a better sense of the way the participants feel about things, about, that is, their internal states. (We also recognize that some people are extremely good actors and actresses who can fool us. That's what actors and actresses do—pretend to have feelings which they don't have and be people who they really aren't.)

This means a kind of game was played in which the television viewers attempted to determine what the people who testified were really like and what they really believed. In playing these games, the viewing audience is always assisted (without recognizing it) by the director. In directing the cameras, the director is also directing the audience.

It is important to remember, then, that the televised version of the hearings was a "mediated" experience, and that the cameras played an important role in shaping the way people responded to the various personalities involved.

The Impact of the Hearings

It is difficult to say what the long-range impact of the hearings will be. During the testimony of Lieutenant Colonel Oliver North there was a brief outburst of what has been described as "Ollie-Mania," and public opinion polls revealed mounting support for the Contra cause. This did not last very long, and a few months after the hearings American public opinion was back where it had been earlier. And all the toy manufacturers and others who hoped to cash in on the North craze found themselves in trouble, with millions of copies of the book of his testimony or millions of Ollie North toy figures in hand.

President Reagan's reputation was severely damaged and many observers believe his lame duck status was accelerated. On the other hand, the American public got a wonderful civics lesson.

Conclusions

I have placed this analysis of the Iran-Contra hearings under the category of hierarchical political cultures because, in essence, we have a story which involves a fight between elements in our political hierarchies and a dispute over the domains of various elites within these hierarchies. We might see this story as involving a battle between what Wildavsky has termed *hierarchical collectivists* (the members of Congress) and *competitive individualists*, North, Hakim, Secord, and the others in the administration who, it is alleged, tried to evade American foreign policy laws ("prescriptions") that Congress had made.

The tension that exists between the hierarchical collectivists and the competitive individualists pervades American politics and culture. It can probably never be resolved, having its origins, I believe, in the psyche and the continual war that exists between the id and the super-ego, between those elements in our psyches that push us to focus on our own desires and wishes and those that tell us to obey the rules of the group and think of the common welfare.

This is one of the tensions that has made American society and the American personality so dynamic—and so unstable. There are other tensions as well, such as the ones between the competitive individualists and the egalitarians and the hierarchical elitists and the fatalists. I will deal with these in the analyses to come.

MTV . . . effaces history in the aesthetic sense of piling together, without acknowledgment, film genres and art movements from different historical periods. Video artists draw freely on the gothic, noir, Western, horror, Science Fiction and thriller film and literary genres, on German Expressionism, French Surrealism, Dada, American folk songs and pop art, etc. The stance of the texts is again that, in the realm of aesthetics, there is one continuous time in which all exists.

> *—E.Ann Kaplan, "History, the Historical Spectator and Gender Address in Music Television."*

MTV is orgasm—when signifiers explode in pleasure in the body in an excess of the physical. No ideology, no social control can organize an orgasm. Only freedom can. All orgasms are democratic: all ideology is autocratic. This is the politics of pleasure. The signifiers work through the senses on the body to produce pleasure and freedom: the signifieds produce sense in the mind for ideology and control. Let us oppose them structurally (as well as politically):

MTV	TV
Signifier	Signified
The Senses	Sense
Body	Mind
Pleasure	Ideology
Freedom	Control
Resistance	Conformity

—John Fiske, "MTV: Post-Structural Post-Modern."

4

Funky Fornication on MTV: *Sledgehammer*

Enigmas

How are we to come to grips with music television? It remains an enigma for a number of reasons. There is, unquestionably, some extremely experimental and interesting video work being done. Yet most MTV is ultimately as boring and banal as the music it illustrates. For every great work there are endless numbers of nondescript hack-work. We might say the same about the novel or any genre, for that matter. Most works of art are, at best, rather ordinary.

But how is it that trashy music is so often transmogrified into something so arty?

Does television merely *illustrate* the song or does the song serve as a secondary element, overwhelmed by the visual power of the video screen and the various special effects that can be generated on video? Have the new video synthesizers turned hacks into auteurs?

If you turn off the sound and watch music television (instead of watching and listening to it) you find it terribly unsatisfying, and often rather silly. It is something like watching a film without sound, except that often in films you can get some idea of what is going on because of the narrative conventions found in most films.

On the other hand, if you don't watch the screen and just listen to the music, it is much more satisfying, especially if you are listening to the video on a high-fidelity television set. This is like listening to the radio. When you put the music and the video together, however, I believe it is the video that dominates. Perhaps this is because television is a cool medium which demands a great deal of ''participation'' on the part of viewers, while radio (and sound) is a hot medium, which doesn't make strong demands on listeners. Could it be that music videos, in McLuhan's terms, are hybrids—hot and cool, tribal and rational (or would it be postrational)?

The Dream Displaced (and Like Soup, Condensed)?

MTV has been described as dreamlike because of its nonlinearity and the fantastic imagery one finds in so many of the videos. There is a great deal of quick cutting, there is the use of flashbacks and flashforwards, there are all kinds of special effects. Isn't it strange that lyrics that are often moronic and repetitive generate such avant-garde, postmodernist visual images. This raises the question of the relationship that exists between the people who write the songs and the people who perform them (often the same people) and the people who create the videos that evolve out of the songs. Who is the auteur?

Saying that music videos are dreamlike implies a methodology for analyzing them which I will use in discussing *Sledgehammer*. We are certainly in a realm where continuity is not of great concern, in a realm where stream of consciousness is important and random associations, incredible displacements, and bizarre condensations assault us and where the right side of the brain, the wholistic, lyrical, magical side dominates.

Dear Genre Letters

There is a question about what music videos are. It strikes me that they are a television genre, much like soap operas or game shows or science fiction shows. That is, they are a kind of television program. But they are also hybrids of sorts, since they are commercials for themselves. And, as might be expected of commercials, they show the same kind of technical mastery and brilliance we find in the best commercials—all in the interest of the sell.

Stimulate desire. Is that not the aim of advertising? Use sexuality and anything else you can to sell. Stimulate desire and provide a means for satisfying it. Beneath the patina of hip rebellion, despite the wild looks and wild lives of the musicians and all the nose-thumbing they do at the squares in society, we find the bourgeois imperative. Sell a million and make a million.

Music videos also suffer from the afflictions of commercials. They are amusing and entertaining, but after a while we get really tired of them. In addition there is the matter of clutter. After you see an evening's worth of television, the commercials get all mixed up with one another in our memory. They merge into one megacommercial. The same applies to videos. After you see enough of them, clutter and information overload take their toll and we end up with one mixed-up megavideo swimming around in our heads.

Many of the bands realize this and recognize that they may be suffering from overexposure and a corresponding underappreciation, so they stop making music videos. In addition, there is the notorious short attention span of teenagers and their endless quest for new sensations.

Analytic Considerations

Well, how do we come to terms with music videos? Let me suggest a number of matters that might be considered in an analysis of a music video. I might point out that a text can be quite simple and seem to be straightforward (or even banal, as I suggested earlier) and yet be connected to very complex psychological phenomena. And just as it is necessary to know something about dreamers to interpret their dreams, it is necessary to know something about American culture (and perhaps Western culture, in general—even Eastern culture and other cultures) to interpret these mass-mediated daydreams. The more you know, the more you see (and understand).

Let me list some of the things we might think about.

1. The lyrics of the song and what they reflect—the language, the metaphors, the rhymes, etc.
2. The beat of the music, its harmonic structure, etc.
3. The performance skills of the musicians.
4. The film techniques used: montage, flashbacks, etc.
5. The story created to illustrate the song (when appropriate).
6. The use of theatrical effects and various special effects.
7. The connections with other works of art (intertextualities).
8. The use of symbols.
9. The use of lighting, color, camera angles, etc.
10. The quality of imagination of the director of the video.
11. The relation of the text to social, political, etc. concerns.

12. The use of condensation, displacement, etc.
13. The persona of the singer(s).

This list suggests that music videos are complex art forms that require a considerable amount of effort to explicate, especially the good ones, where we find wonderful songs allied with superb performances by musicians in inventive narratives that are brilliantly produced. There is nothing in the genre that says we cannot have brilliant videos, but there is a great deal of poverty of imagination in musicians and video creators which tells us we won't have many.

In this study I do not wish to deal with the genre; there have been a number of excellent studies of music video per se. Instead, I wish to offer an analysis of a particular text—*Sledgehammer*, by Peter Gabriel, to see what it reflects about the contemporary scene.

Sledgehammer Synopsis

It is impossible to capture the complexity of this music video (or any music video, for that matter) in words. Let me however offer a brief and highly simplified account of what transpires in this most confusing and confounding text.

The video starts with a shot of sperm moving about. Then we see something that looks like cells and a cell that has been fertilized (?) followed by what seems to be blood flowing in veins or arteries. It pulses back and forth, in rhythm with the music. We see an eyeball. The pupil grows large (dilates) and then returns to normal size. This is followed by extreme close-ups of a finger, a lip, an earlobe (which also moves to the beat of the music) and an eye that blinks, a mouth, and finally a full face shot of Peter Gabriel. His face twitches spastically.

Then we see a steam train circling around his head which is followed by an airplane, made of paper, clouds, and blue sky. Gabriel's face is colored blue, but his mouth is left in flesh tones. A megaphone covers his mouth. He uses the megaphone. Next he is on an imaginary rollercoaster (represented by drawings behind him and the way his hair flies around).

The scene shifts to bumpercars with popcorn in the background. Do we see cotton candy on his head? The bumpercars bump into Gabriel's head from each side. Next we see his head upside down on the screen.

The scene reverts to normal and we see a body with a head that grows out of ice. A sledgehammer breaks the ice and reveals a face. A fish enters the figure's left ear and a number of smaller ones exit the right ear. Then two fishes enter his head, one from each ear.

We now come to a scene in which fruit jump around and eventually form a human face. Next wooden objects appear and jump around, eventually covering most of Gabriel's face. This leads to clay animation. A clay face (Gabriel's) is shown and a body emerges out of the face. The hands of the clay figure become sledgehammers.

Various images flash on the screen, some of which resemble Jackson Pollock paintings. A Yin-Yang symbol is shown, each part of which turns into a fish and swims away. We see a sledgehammer hit a stage, leaving an egg. The egg becomes a chicken which starts dancing. The chicken becomes two chickens which dance. They leap up in the air.

We now enter the "kick the habit" scene. Here Gabriel sings and we see a number of black women backing him up. A television set with what seems to be Gabriel's mouth, moving, is seen. Gabriel is now surrounded by many figures from many races. People and objects now move around very quickly and Gabriel becomes surrounded and perhaps trapped by these objects. Finally he sits down, the chair turns around and he looks out at a star-filled sky. He is made of stars, also. He gets up, lurches forward, leaves the room and merges with the starry universe. The video ends.

Poetic Licentiousness

Let us imagine a discussion between a person interested in the symbolic significance of some of the allusions in the song and Dr. Sigmund Freud, the father of psychoanalysis and the person who opened up the analysis of dreams with his masterpiece on the interpretation of dreams.

Person: What do you make of the first two lines which talk about a person having a steam train if the person would lay down tracks.

Freud: If you recall my analysis in chapter 10 of *A General Introduction to Psycho-Analysis* of symbols, you will remember that I suggested that objects which are long and upstanding like sticks, umbrellas, poles, and trees are representations of the penis. Also objects that penetrate. Trains are obviously phallic symbols and a train going into a tunnel is, in a camouflaged way, a representation of intercourse. "Laying down tracks" has an obvious meaning here.

Person: What about the airplane flying in the next line? Are airplanes sexual symbols?

Freud: Recall that I talked about the property of the penis being able to raise itself upright, in defiance of the law of gravity, which is part of the phenomenon known as erection. We find, then, this is represented symbolically by balloons, planes, Zeppelins, etc.

Person: I won't even ask you about the mention of the Big Dipper, going up and down and all around. That seems pretty obvious to me. Would the reference to bumper cars be a modified example of what you said about trains? The song talks about bumping and suggests the amusement never will end.

Freud: Your analysis makes sense.

Person: But what does it mean when the singer says he wants to be "your sledgehammer"?

Freud: A sledgehammer is also a phallic symbol. I had suggested that objects from which water flows and objects which are capable of elongation are phallic symbols—but so are pencils, penholders, nail-files, hammers, and other implements which tend to be long and thin and thus vaguely resemble the penis. A sledgehammer would be a very powerful phallic symbol—perhaps representing an overdeveloped sexual drive?

Person: Let's move on to the line in which the singer asks to be shown around his object's fruitcage and suggests he will be her honeybee?

Freud: Here we are dealing with sex again. The breasts and the larger hemispheres of the human body are represented by apples, peaches, and fruit in general. Fruit is full of seeds and thus fruit is vaguely analogous to the female, who has the like capacity to reproduce.

Person: So when the singer talks about opening up your fruitcage, there is an implicit sexual aspect to the request.

Freud: Definitely. The female genitalia are represented symbolically by all objects which share the property with them of enclosing space or being capable of acting as receptacles. We are talking about such things as pits, hollows, caves, jars, bottles, boxes—and here fruitcages, a doubly sexual allusion.

Person: Is it possible that when the singer talks about shedding his skin he is talking about having sex without using a condom? The term skin is a slang expression for condoms.

Freud: That seems a reasonable hypothesis.

Person: So when going dancing in, that too is about sexual intercourse?

Freud: Quite likely. As I suggested in my book, rhythmical activities such as dancing, riding, and climbing are representations of sexual intercourse. Remember that we use symbols to mask things and displace something we find difficult to deal with, psychologically speaking, with something that represents it but does not generate feelings of guilt. When we dream about being on trains that go into tunnels, we are dreaming about sexual intercourse, but we have disguised the dream so it doesn't attract the attention of our superego and cause problems.

Person: So all the talk about the singer's lover feeling the power in her, asking her to "come on, help me do," suggesting that they will be feeding the rhythm day and night . . . all this is about sex. And the song is really a highly erotic, disguised song about sexual intercourse among people who seem to be hypersexed? All this, however, is hidden (at least to a certain degree) in a song that seems to be rather silly, dealing with sledgehammers and such.

Freud: You might also notice that the word "testimony" which is used in the song is very close to the word "testes" and almost certainly was used to suggest, in the unconscious of the listener, that reference.

Person: When we listen to that song do we recognize all this? How do we get the message? When I first heard it I could see that there were some sexual allusions, but I didn't get everything.

Freud: That is because much of communication is at a level below our awareness and involves the unconscious. As I have consistently pointed out, we have an unconscious, and it is often affected by phenomenon which we are unaware of . . . which communicate or speak from the unconscious of the artist to our unconscious. We are often affected by this communication in profound ways, but we do not realize what generated the reactions we have.

Person: One might think, from *Sledgehammer*, that sexuality was a preoccupation of everyone . . . that it is the center of their being.

Freud: You said it, I didn't!

The Visual Aspects of *Sledgehammer*

This text is so complicated and so full of fascinating visuals that I could write a book about the video and still not cover everything. Let me, instead, focus on some of the more striking and important visuals shown.

In Table 4.1 I identify the visual image found in the text, say something about how it communicates (from a semiotic perspective), and speculate about its meaning, or what it communicates. This table is somewhat reductionistic, but it is impossible to talk about visual images and what they communicate without some simplifying.

Table 4.1 indicates, rather clearly, that much of the symbology in the video involves sexuality, birth, reproduction, fertility, and related concerns. And that much of the communication is indirect via symbols and representations that suggest their meaning but don't spell it out.

What is curious is that when you see *Sledgehammer*, it seems to be a somewhat zany, crazy, innocent video. Gabriel gives no indication, via facial expression or gesture, that the subject of the video is sex. It seems almost goofy. There is also no significant other shown. He sings to some kind of imaginary other, and there is no sexploitation of the female body to be seen.

There is one scene that is interesting from an historical point of view, and that is the one where the fruit forms a face. This reminds me of the Italian artist Archimboldo, who made paintings in which human beings were represented by collections of fruit and vegetables. These paintings were optical illusions, and the scene in *Sledgehammer* might be understood as an example of what semioticians describe as intertextuality. This term refers to the fact that all texts are related to all other texts and that artists draw upon history in creating their works, whether on a conscious level or not.

TABLE 4.1
Symbology and Meaning of Sledgehammer

Visual	Method of Communication	Meaning
sperm	iconic	reproduction
sledgehammer	iconic	phallus
train	iconic/metaphoric	phallus
roller coaster	iconic/metaphoric	phallus
eggs	symbolic	fertility
plane	symbolic	phallus
fruit	symbolic	fertility
dilated retina	indexical	sexual arousal
dancing	symbolic	intercourse
door	symbolic	female genitals
chickens	symbolic	human beings

The visuals seem to suggest an evolutionary development which takes the following sequence: sperm, cells, eggs, parts of head, face, body, society, universe. I have to ask myself whether something of this sort occurred to the creator of this text or whether this is something imposed by my mind, seeking to make sense of this maddening video. Did I create order out of chaos? Are the dancing featherless chickens those "featherless bipeds" philosophers talk about all the time?

A Marxist Reading

Is it possible to see Peter Gabriel, the hero of this mixed-up and confusing little story, as a typically alienated figure in a dehumanizing bourgeois society? From the Marxist perspective, Gabriel's hypersexuality would be interpreted as being generated by the inhuman society in which he finds himself. He is a good lumpen proletariat figure, with no ties to anyone, who takes out his self-loathing and anger in incessant sexual activity. This behavior is analogous to that of rats in certain laboratory experiments.

Our hero is animated but there is little vitality to him or in the video. Animation is an attempt to give inanimate objects life, but there is something wrong with this: the animated figures and objects aren't alive and there is something perverse about the way they are made to jump around.

Might animation be a metaphor for life in bourgeois capitalist societies where people have the illusion that they are in control of their lives and destinies but, in fact, they are only objects manipulated by others? In such a situation, is the commodity fetishism of the last scenes, in which furniture and other objects pile into the room that Gabriel occupies, almost smothering him, until he escapes via some sort of death and identification with the starry universe? Sexual lust and consumer lust, Marxists argue, are the twin engines that drive bourgeois societies and help alienated proletarians delude themselves into believing they have power (other than the ability to procreate) and meaningful lives. *Sledgehammer* reveals a great deal about capitalist bourgeois societies, and the message it sends is far removed from the message it thinks it is sending.

One might extend the argument and say that music videos and the whole entertainment-communication industry in bourgeois societies is devoted to deluding people, making them forget about the economic relations that exist in their societies and their true situation. These videos, advertisements for themselves, push the logic of bourgeois societies to their final conclusion . . . solipsistic, nihilistic self-aggrandizement for the purpose of delusion and profit but at the cost of alienation.

Final Thoughts

In this text there is a split between biology and technology that is pretty pervasive. There is sperm and there is a representation of sperm, a sledgehammer. There is the real face of Gabriel and there is the animated face made out of fruit. There is real movement, when Gabriel dances, and there is animated movement, when the chickens dance or the figure made of wooden sticks dances.

The problem we find in analyzing videos such as *Sledgehammer* is that technology seems to have outstripped imagination and now that video makers can do almost anything, they are making texts in which the technology seems to have taken control. I find *Sledgehammer* boring. It obviously took a great deal of technological ability to make and is an interesting example of what can be done using the new technologies. But I find it somewhat lifeless and irritating; it made me work very hard and at the end I didn't think it was worth the effort.

It has a good beat and it is full of sex—two of the basic requirements, I imagine, for a successful music video. It also has a comic, zany quality that I rather like, which does a good job of masking what the song and video are really about. You find *that* out when you read the lyrics or listen carefully to them.

What bothers me most, probably, is that, somehow, the text is lifeless and cold. This may be the result of technological overkill? *Sledgehammer* speaks of love but with ice-cold breath and a frozen heart.

Science has at last turned its attention to the central question of human capability, has begun the search for a technology as well as a science of the human potential. Men in varied fields, sometimes unknown to each other, sometimes disagreeing on method, philosophy and even language, are coming to startlingly similar conclusions that make pessimism about the human prospect far more difficult than before. These men—neurologists, psychologists, educators, philosophers and others—are making what may well be the century's biggest news. Almost all of them agree that people now are using less than ten percent of their potential abilities; some put the figure at less than one percent. The fact of the matter is that anyone *who makes a responsible and systematic study of the human animal eventually feels the awe that moved Shakespeare to write: "What a piece of work is man! how noble in reason! how infinite in faculty!"*

    —George B. Leonard, Education and Ecstasy

5

Be All That You Can Buy: The Human Potential Movement in Marin County

Marvelous Marin

This is a personal investigation of the Human Potential Movement in Marin County, which lies just north of the Golden Gate Bridge. I've lived in Mill Valley, a town of about 15,000 people, since 1970 and like other Marinites, I have observed various aspects of the human potential movement with a kind of bemused fascination. Marin County, which might be described as the vortex of the movement, was once known as "marvelous uptight Marin," because it was supposedly full of rather square, conventional (and therefore "repressed") business types who were attracted by its beauty and proximity to San Francisco —and who could afford to live there.

That description of Marin changed, suddenly, and it became quite famous as the "I want it all now" county, which is how a nationally broadcast television documentary characterized it. That is, the county was portrayed as full of affluent, hedonistic, "me-decade" types (or might I say "me-decadent") who spent their time soaking in redwood hot tubs, trying to decide which wrinkle in the human potential movement to experiment with next.

The excesses of the movement were wittily satirized in Cyra McFadden's book, *The Serial*, which first appeared as weekly installments in a Marin County free newspaper, *The Pacific Sun*. The book was made into a film which, though it got poor reviews, helped cement the image of Marin County into people's minds.

It was in Marin County that something called "Mind Dynamics" was born and this, in turn, led to several of the more prominent human potential organizations such as EST (Erhard seminar training) and Lifespring and Actualizations. EST was born when a man named Jack Rosenberg was driving on highway 101 in Marin and got "it," becoming transmogrified (in the process) into Werner Erhard.

George Leonard lives in Mill Valley; he is one of the writers who is most closely associated with the human potential movement and with humanistic psychology. There are countless other writers, psychologists, therapists, and gurus of one sort or another who also live in Marin County.

The place is literally crawling with people offering training, help, or workshops in Alexander Technique, biofeedback, bioenergetics, NLP (neuro-linguistic programming), Rolfing, massage (Swedish, Shiatsu, etc.), sex therapy, wellness training, holistic health, Samadhi tanks, mental "off court" tennis training, wilderness experiences, Tragering, acupressure, sand tray experiences, t'ai chi ch'uan, mud baths, hatha yoga, love addiction, eating disorders, incest problems and so on. I should mention one more thing: Marin County is one of the wealthiest counties in America. Realizing one's potential, it turns out, is not cheap, but many Marinites believe it is worth whatever it costs.

The Pacific Sun

When I decided to investigate the human potential movement I turned to *The Pacific Sun* to get an idea of what services were available. At one time *The Pacific Sun* charged for subscriptions, but now it is a give-away paper. It prints some 30,000 copies each week and covers all of Marin County. (Each week it has a focus on a different topic: the family, food and drink, health and fitness, and home/fashion/cars and travel.) I checked the display and classified advertisements for individuals or organizations that might fit into the rough category of human potential and found advertisements for the various services listed above.

At times it is difficult to decide where the "human potential" ends and something else, such as psychiatric help or conventional medical assistance begins. If you define the human potential movement as involving alternative or nontraditional ways of treating people who have medical, psychological, or relational problems (as well as other difficulties that further cloud the issue) you get a tolerably useful way of making distinctions.

If you read *The Pacific Sun* for a while you discover that there are a bewildering variety of mindworkers and bodyworkers who cater to the needs, whims, and desires of just about anyone who is interested in fulfilling his or her potential in any way he or she might wish.

Interviewing Practitioners

I visited a physical therapy center in Mill Valley and spoke with its director. Half of the business of the center is devoted to traditional physical therapy and the other half to massage, exercise rooms, hot tubs, and saunas. When I asked the director why the human potential movement was flourishing, he said it was connected to several factors: first, a swing against traditional medicine, which he felt was limited, and second, to a great deal of narcissism.

I asked him how one separates the frauds and charlatans from legitimate practitioners and he became very animated. "Lots of people," he said, "have a healer syndrome . . . have a need to be healers and have fantasies that they have talents or powers." He was particularly upset about some massage parlors that claim to be physical therapy centers but don't have licensed physical therapists. But he didn't provide a satisfactory answer to my question. Once you get beyond credentialed physical therapists, how do you know you're not (literally) in the hands of a fake?

That is the crucial question and one that nobody in the human potential movement could answer. Many people, who would identify themselves as within the movement, said that if a person undergoing some treatment or therapy "felt" that he or she was being helped, that was enough.

I went to another "therapy center" which, it turned out, did not have licensed therapists. When I asked the manager about this, he hemmed and hawed and finally said something about massages being therapeutic, though no "real" physical therapy, with licensed therapists, per se, was conducted on the premises. I asked him whether he gave massages. "No," he replied. "I do bodywork, but I'm too expensive for this place." "What exactly do you do?" I asked? "Structural release and alignment . . . at my place," he answered.

He said he had learned this art as an apprentice and had been doing it for eight years. "We're into nature and the body here," he continued. "Traditional medicine has gone high-tech."

As I chatted with him, he was busy calling some credit bureau to check on the credit ratings of two patrons who had just come in to use the hot tubs. He showed me the schedule for his place: they give seven or eight massages a day and make most of their money from their hot tubs. "Most of the people who want massages call up just a while before . . . it seems to be a spur of the moment kind of thing."

On the Marginality of Therapy Centers

From the various discussions I had I came away with a strong sense of the marginality of most of the "practitioners" and with the notion that much of what goes on in the human potential movement is really a form of entertainment.

Not only is a good deal of the human potential movement involved with popular culture (through its use of advertising and its role as the object of endless satires), it *is* popular culture. It is most useful to see all the different therapists, experts, practitioners, etc. in the human potential movement as entertainers, if one wishes to be charitable, and the movement as a kind of theatre of the therapeutic absurd.

Lingua Potentialica

Human potential practitioners have developed numerous jargons that have the function of separating them from others and of giving them an identity (and kind of pseudo-status). In some cases, as in EST, people who undergo the training learn a number of words which they use in special ways. (These trainees are described by those hostile to EST, as EST-holes.)

To understand the significance of Lingua Potentialica, I've listed some of the basic terms and placed opposite them words or phrases from what might be called Lingua Actualica. I'm not sure what the opposite of potentiality is: is it actuality (which stresses what is rather than what might be) or reactionary (which stresses what was rather than what might be)?

Lingua Potentialica	Lingua Actualica
grounded	up-in-the-air
centered	going off on tangents
balanced	unstable
holistic	specialized
harmonious	discordant
sharing	self-centered
caring	indifferent
exploring	narrow minded

This language implies two different orientations to life. One is based on the natural and is concerned with "inner-space" and all the remarkable things the body and mind are capable of doing. The other is based on culture and "outer space" and focuses on high technology, specialization, and traditions stemming from science and scientific method.

If I were to suggest two figures that best symbolize the difference between these two perspectives, imagine, first, someone lying in Samadhi tank, cut off to the extent it is possible, from bodily sensation and the outside world and almost totally immersed in his or her "inner space." The other figure would be an astronaut, hurtling through outer space and connected to the world by billions of dollars of technology: rockets, computers, devices monitoring bodily functions, and television cameras.

It is ironic that the human potential movement and the Space Program developed at approximately the same time. It may be that the national preoccupation with outer space led many to turn their attention in the opposite direction. When America sent a man to the moon, we provided the world with a $25 billion television media event—a "special" to end "specials" (as television programs used to be called).

One question we might consider is this: to what degree is the human potential movement also a form of entertainment (extreme narrowcasting to use the television jargon) in which we have turned from science fiction and space operas to their opposite (the mysteries of India? the occult?) and developed a new form or genre of autobiography? Did not Montaigne write "I study myself more than any other subject. That is my metaphysics, that is my physics." And speaking of metaphysics and physics, colonic irrigation has become important lately and so have metaphysical discussion groups and psychics.

One finds large numbers of people speaking what has been described as *psychobabble*—which is the title of a book about "fast talk and quick cure in the era of feeling" by R.D. Rosen. Psychobabble is a melange of jargon from the human potential movement and related areas. People speak psychobabble when they talk about "getting in touch with themselves," their need for "space," getting their "act together," and becoming "whole," their need for more meaningful "relationships," and so on.

This psychobabble is significant, Rosen argues, because it "facilitates a belief in the immediate availability of well-being" and suggests that "psychological growth may be achieved through an act of will" (Rosen 1977, 13). It tends to delude people and give them unrealistic expectations.

There are, it could be argued, societal pressures and forces which have the ultimate affect of pushing people towards the human potential movement. Why these forces affect some groups and not others remains a puzzle, but it might have something to do with income level as well as the cultural pressures—or is it subcultural pressures—in Marin County. Marin is very wealthy but it also has a great deal of alcoholism and an extremely high suicide rate.

Symbology of the Movement

In an effort to attain some kind of an identity and to differentiate themselves from their numerous competitors, many of the organizations and practitioners in the human potential movement have developed logos. The best place to find these organizations and their logos is in a give-away publication, *Commonground*, which deals with "resources for personal transformation" and which is distributed in the Bay Area.

The purposes of *Commonground* is to provide "access to resources," and it is meant to be used, so it says, as a "directory rather than a guide or handbook." It has advertisements for such services as the arts, healing and bodywork, lifework and passages, the psychic arts and intuitive "sciences," psychology, therapy, and spiritual practices.

A typical issue has approximately sixty pages of advertisements (and a few pages or so of text). Most pages in this tabloid have display advertisements for eight or nine entities (generally each has a logo) though *Commonground* also carries a large number of nondisplay advertisements—similar in nature to what we find in the classified section of a newspaper. A typical issue carries notices and advertisements, then, for something like 500 different practitioners and organizations, which gives you a good idea of how many people are involved in the human potential movement and peripheral areas such as alternative universities, chiropractors, and holistic clinics.

Many of these logos are based on circles and, in particular, variations of the Yin-Yang symbol. Hands, mandala-like figures, waves, oriental letters, triangles, and mystical figures are also quite popular. Yin and Yang are complementary opposites and are associated, by most people, with the Orient, China, and by implication Chinese folk medicine. Yin reflects negativity, darkness, and the feminine while Yang reflects the opposite of these, namely positiveness, light, and the masculine. The interaction of these two forces allegedly influences our destinies.

This symbol has relevance for the human potential movement since it suggests the need to integrate mind and body, the physical and the spiritual, to achieve some kind of physical and psychic balance.

Mr. Human Potential: George Leonard

George Leonard is the author of *Education and Ecstasy*, *The Transformation*, *The Ultimate Athlete*, and many other books. He writes, teaches aikido at a dojo he owns with two partners, and is president of the Association for Humanistic Psychology, which is headquartered in San Francisco. I've known him for a number of years and he was kind enough to spend an afternoon with me talking about the human potential movement.

"Early in 1964," he said, "I wrote an article for *Look* magazine (he was the West coast editor of the magazine until it folded) called 'The Revolution in Education.' It dealt with programmed instruction. At that time I was fashionably cynical about human possibility and was, like many, more concerned about 'how to be unhappy with style.' In the last paragraph of the article I discussed my feelings about human possibility and said something about human potential. I got a lot of mail about that article and most of it was about the last paragraph . . . and that got me interested.

"I then decided to do a major piece on the human potential movement for *Look* and spent the next six months interviewing people all over the country—psychologists, brain researchers, educators, etc. I eventually wrote a long 20,000 word piece that I thought *Look* would use in two parts. But they turned it down saying it was too technical. I had interviewed something like forty people and was trying to put together, one way or another, the thinking of Carl Rogers and B.F. Skinner.

"In February of 1965 I met Mike Murphy, who had started Esalen in 1962, and we really clicked. Mike knew about Eastern philosophy and disciplines and I knew about Western behavioral thought, politics, and brain research . . . that kind of thing. I ended up doing a lot for Esalen on the side, while I continued working for *Look*. Much of our thought in the movement stems, indirectly, from a talk Aldous Huxley gave in 1961 called 'Human Potentiality.' It deals with the need for education in the nonverbal humanities, for ways of developing affect and other things like that which had been neglected.

"Nineteen sixty-five through 1966 were exciting times at Esalen. We had the 'star system' in operation then—with people like Carl Rogers, B.F. Skinner, and Paul Tillich there. This was the period of the Civil Rights movement and it was only natural that we saw things in terms of movements. Early in 1966 Mike and I brainstormed a great deal and we thought up the idea of having a residential program at Esalen. It would be a highly structured program lasting nine months and students would present a thesis or tape, something like that. Virginia Satir was one of the people associated with us then.

"In 1967–1968 Will Schutz took over. He had all the credentials anyone could want. . . . Well it turned out that he was totally committed to encounters as a means towards breaking through into new understandings of oneself, etc. He skewed the program into that area. Fritz Perls was there also . . . and there was a bit of rivalry between them as to whom [*sic*] was to be the star. Ida Rolf also spent some time there."

I asked him what he thought about the way the media covered the human potential movement.

"The media has been awful," he replied. "One of the earliest pieces was quite favorable. Leo Litwak, a professor at San Francisco State University, got an assignment from *The New York Times Magazine* to do a piece on Esalen. He went down there quite skeptical, spent five days in one of Schutz's encounter groups, and had a profound experience. So he wrote "Joy is the Prize," which was published on December 31, 1967. The piece won many awards and has been anthologized numerous times. It was the right kind of piece . . . he started off with misgivings and then was turned around.

"Then came a flood of articles and books by people who really didn't understand the human potential movement and made an equation between it and small groups and then between small groups and encounter groups. That's not the case at all. You have to realize the role *The New York Times* plays in all this. The 'reality check' for Madison Avenue and the whole East Coast is *The New York Times*, which, in the sixties, was enormously influential. It still is. *The New York Times* asked Cyra McFadden to write a piece on the human potential movement and her main credential for writing about it was that she admittedly has had nothing to do with it.

"Many of the so-called experts on the subject know nothing about it and their scholarship in their writing is abominable. A lot of people who write about it have not had any experiences in the human potential field nor have they spoken with any of the people in it. People quote others who know nothing about it themselves. And sometimes they print damned lies. It isn't true, for example, as *The Village Voice* alleges, that Mike Murphy created Esalen so he could make a lot of money. He gave Esalen land worth millions. Just the opposite is true, as a matter of fact.

"Then, on the other side, there were all those gushy articles that made the human potential movement look even worse. They did a lot of damage, gave people a silly idea of what the human potential movement is about, and attracted the wrong kind of people into it. One thing about the human potential movement is that it lends itself to parody."

"I notice that myself," I said. "And it's hard to resist, I guess. But why do you think the East Coast is so negative?"

"Because we represent a threat to them . . . and their hegemony over human perceptions. We represent a different set of values and a different way of perceiving the world. And our ideas have had a great deal of influence on the seventies. My book, *The Transformation*, has recently been re-issued. When it appeared a dozen years ago, nobody knew what I was talking about. Now I'd say it is mainstream.

"There's a huge invisible constituency out there now, even if the East Coast establishment still sees us as 'fair game.' It seems like every time an East Coast editor sees a term like 'zen' or 'transformation' or 'human potential' or even 'California' they dismiss the rules about copy checking and fact checking and think only in terms of ridicule and spoofing."

"What about the criticism that people in the human potential movement are self-absorbed, narcissistic and very much part of the 'me generation'?" I asked.

"Most of the people in the human potential movement are not a-political or narcissistic. The people who go to Esalen are probably more concerned about social and political matters than others. In 1967, for example, Price Cobbs and I did the first black-white marathon encounter. You have to realize that I come from the South and did a lot of work for *Look* on the Civil Rights movement."

"How do you explain the election of Ronald Reagan if people are living by the new values that stem from the human potential movement?

He laughed.

"Reagan represents a widespread resentment against bigness and centralization. These matters are quite close to transformational values. That's part of the story."

It was late in the afternoon and time for him to lead a class in energy awareness and then teach aikido at his dojo. He invited me to attend the class and participate in it, which I did. There were about twenty-five people of all ages and we performed various exercises. He explained what he was trying to do and generally acted as a kindly and understanding teacher. We were asked to move to the center of the huge mat that covered most of the room and do some exercises with a partner who we "found" though our eyes were closed.

It was completely foreign to my experience and way of thinking, yet, after he explained what he was doing, I could see the sense of it. After an hour of energy-awareness exercises the aikido class began. People started throwing themselves and others around, slamming the mat as they fell, bowing to one another, and learning various moves from Leonard. Tall and slender, he looked like a wonderfully graceful stork as he "glided" among the various bodies who were tossing one another about. Every so often he would clap his hands and the students would stop what they were doing and hurry to the edge of the mat to learn a new hold or throw.

I could not help but notice the excitement and energy in the room and the pleasure the aikido students got from their work and from their teacher. Leonard wore an aikido costume, the special kind worn by teachers. There seemed to be a strange contradiction at hand: a rather saintly looking man teaching a martial art. Aikido, from what I could observe from the class, is a combination of exercise, mysticism, ritual, dance, therapy, and community meeting that seems to cater to the varying needs of its adherents quite nicely.

The Problem of Legitimacy

As a result of my interview with Leonard I found myself in a quandry—still unable to separate the legitimate people in the human potential movement from the frauds and charlatans. Leonard acknowledged that this was a legitimate problem but suggested that any cure might be worse than the disease itself.

There are, it seems two camps—one made of people of considerable reputation, education, and training who, for one reason or another, find themselves out of the mainstream. And there is another camp of people, attracted to the movement, whose honesty and integrity is suspect. How one separates the wheat from the chaff is the big problem. Most writers take the easy route when they deal with the movement which is parody because they don't take it seriously and don't know how to deal with it.

If Leonard is correct, many people have the wrong idea about the human potential movement. This idea stems from the East Coast he argues, and has been filtered through *The New York Times* and the East Coast media establishment. (I'm not so sure this is so, for in many cases what we find are unwitting self-parodies by the various practitioners who have chosen the human potential movement as a convenient umbrella. It is one thing for writers to parody a movement; it is another thing for members of the movement to parody themselves.) It may be a bit of an oversimplification, but I think we can see a bipolar opposition between the Eastern seaboard and California here that explains most of what I've been discussing.

Polarities Relative to Human Potential Movement	
Eastern Seabord Culture	**California/West Coast Culture**
Medical/psychological	Humanistic, wholistic
Therapeutic Establishment	Human potential movement

High tech/mechanistic	Natural organic/vitalistic
Conservative, rigid	Radical, experimental
Cynical	Utopian
New York Times establishment	Underground, counter-cultural
Media	Media

These two points of view (and everything connected with them) are now fighting it out for controlling the way we perceive our place in the world. Everything from our medical system, educational system, and political order will probably be affected by the way these oppositions are resolved. The battle, Leonard believes, is being won by the West Coast.

Conclusions, Questions, and Considerations of the Human Potential Movement and Popular Culture Among Other Things

Is there something ironic about the human potential movement?

Does "achieving one's potential" put greater pressure on an individual than, say, competing with others out in the "cruel world?" Isn't inner-space endless, and isn't the quest for achievement the cause of many of our problems?"

Has the human potential movement, with its special language and its blend of mysticism and massage created a new American comic figure?

Is the human potential movement still moving?

Or is it petering out and modifying itself so it is hardly recognizable? Is it a fad from California that will eventually be taken up in the Midwest and on the East Coast (and Europe) at the same time that it is being replaced in California by something else?

How do we take what is valuable from the human potential movement and extricate this from all the nonsense and fakery?

Since the human potential movement has its roots in American culture and American values (example: achievement, motivation, and perfectionism), can it be popular elsewhere?

If the human potential movement does spread abroad, is that a sign that Americanization has become widespread and that there have been major changes in values and attitudes that might not have been recognized before? Would such a thing be a good example of American cultural imperialism?

Is massage (and other forms of bodywork associated with the human potential movement) connected to our sense of isolation and loneliness and our need, somehow, to be touched?

If we pay psychiatrists $100 an hour so we can have someone to talk with, why not pay a bodyworker $50 so we can have someone touch us.

Is the human potential movement ultimately some kind of sophisticated pop culture for people who find our contemporary bureaucratic, scientific, post-modern society boring?

Can the human potential movement be described as "Yin and Yankee"?

Is it possible that what is most important about the human potential movement is the impact it is having on traditional medicine and related healing and helping professions?

Are we to judge the human potential movement by its worst examples?

Don't movements all tend to become more moderate as they evolve and also become more respectable? Can the human potential movement ever become conventional and respectable?

After you've achieved your potential, what do you do for an encore?

Max is popular because of his, "In one word: individuality," says Sean Fitzpatrick, executive-vice president/director of creative services for Campbell-Ewald, Warren, Mich.

"The youth market in particular, and the rest of us in general, are scared to death of being homogenized out of existence."

"That's the reason young people go to fashion extremes, and then, when their style gets popular, they go on to other things. Max also tends to articulate things they want to say, but can't for a variety of reasons."

Says Lee deBoer, a senior vice president at Cinemax, "The uniqueness of the character is a category that American audiences have never seen before." DeBoer describes Max as "almost a parody of television."

"As America becomes more and more of a hype television society, the parody works," he says. "The technical side of him may be a novelty in the long run, but the personality will hold audiences."

—*Susan Sewell, "Datebook"* San Francisco Examiner

6

Max Headroom: Adventures of a Disembodied Hero

Preliminary Questions

What are we to make of Max Headroom, perhaps the most interesting new hero on television in recent years, whose exploits seem to have captured the attention of millions of young and not-so-young people (and inspired, one might assume, millions of others to drink more Coca-Cola)? Why does this character have such an appeal? Why do so many people find this disembodied head so intriguing? What does the program reflect about contemporary American society and politics? These are some of the questions I propose to answer in this investigation.

But first, for those who are not familiar with the show, let me recount the plot of the pilot program.

Synopsis of the Pilot Program

The opening story informs us that we are "twenty minutes into the future," and we find ourselves in an Orwellian world in which television shapes the lives of the masses. The television networks are in fierce competition with one another for realtime ratings, which, thanks to the technology of the day, are shown second by second. Edison Carter, the main hero of the program, works as a combination investigative reporter-cameraman, who is aided by a "controller." He works with a computer, traces Carter's activities, and by accessing all kinds of data banks and other kinds of information, guides him and helps him find his way about.

He is asked by the news director to investigate the sudden death of a person, John Q. Public, who exploded, suddenly, while watching television. Just before he discovers what happened, he is told by his "controller" to abandon the story since the network doesn't want him to pursue it. He insists on getting a new controller, and the heroine of the series, Theora Jones, is assigned to him. On his own, more or less, Carter and Jones use her computer to access the building's security cameras and eavesdrop on network executives who are using urinals in an executive bathroom.

They discover that Public exploded while watching a *blipvert*, an intense form of commercial that was designed to prevent people from switching channels. Unfortunately, these blipverts are very dangerous and have the unfortunate side effect of blowing up certain people. The head of the network, an amoral character named Grossberg, refuses to take the blipverts off the air, because if he does he will lose the network's biggest sponsor.

In the futuristic society portrayed in *Max Headroom*, computers are ubiquitous, and the whole society is linked together by them. Jones uses her computer to scan the network and discovers that the blipverts were created by a secret programmer, a kind of genius-nerd boy named Bryce. The network, which has discovered what Carter is up to, has its security forces search for him. He attempts to escape on a motorcycle but runs head-on into a barrier that warns about "Maximum Head-room."

The network leaders assume Carter is dying. They want to find out how much he knew, and at their behest Bryce finds a way to copy Carter's memory into a computer. Carter is then sent off to a body bank, where parts of human beings are salvaged for various uses. Carter's memory takes the form of a face, a stylized version of Carter's, whose first words recall Carter's last thought—when he saw the sign Max(imum) Headroom. Thus Max Headroom, a smart-alecky, wise-cracking, comic character, comes into being. His first words are "M-m-m-m-max Headroom." He does not stutter but seems to have minor problems finding the right word.

Jones is able to find the body bank where Carter was brought, discovers that he is alive, and arranges to save him. He is nursed back to health by her and is to team up with her and his alter ego, Max, to crusade against the evils of their society. Max Headroom, meanwhile, has escaped somehow into the computer system and is beyond the control of the network. He has the power, also to put himself on television and his appearances are a great success, it turns out, and the ratings go up.

"Do you want to know how to tell when a network president is lying?" asks Max. "His lips move." As a result of Max, the blipverts are taken off the air, Grossberg loses his job, and a team of crusaders for justice is born: Edison Carter, Max Headroom, Theora Jones, and Bryce, the boy computer genius.

Max as a Culture Hero

Why should this disembodied head and the various characters assembled around it have such resonance? Why has the program attracted a cult following? For one thing, Max is a comic figure and many people find his wisecracks and general insouciance entertaining. He is a joker and perhaps even a clown figure—and like fools, his remarks often strike at the heart of a given situation.

Equally important, I think, is the fact that he stands for freedom in a system that seems all-powerful and permeates every aspect of society. The series posits a world that has a very authoritarian, if not totalitarian, political system. Yet, even in this world, there is room, Max shows us, for people (or is it characters) to find ways of being free, of escaping from domination and of holding up powerful people and institutions to the one thing they cannot abide—public ridicule.

It is this aspect of Max Headroom that is so appealing to young people, I believe. He is a model for them and the program is a kind of metaphor expressing their feelings—their fear of being controlled, in one way or another, by unsympathetic individuals and institutions. Max Headroom is a free spirit, and young people can identify with him in this respect. But he, too, is a prisoner—of the electronic circuits that he exists in, for he is, in the final analysis, only an image, and his freedom is not by any means absolute.

Max Headroom is an id figure with a superego function. In this respect, he also has relevance for young people, who must struggle with their ids and who would like to think that satisfying their drives is a good thing and a nice way of improving society. His superego mirrors that of the person he was created from—Edison Carter. The dominant ego figure in the series is Theora Jones, who uses her computers to obtain information of all kinds, information that people often try to keep hidden. But Carter, himself, as an investigative reporter, is also an ego figure. (Neither she nor Edison Carter lack sexual drives, which are directed more and more towards one another as the series progresses.)

One questions that arises is whether Max Headroom, being only an electronic image, represents *true* independence and rebelliousness or only the image of it. When young people identify with Max Headroom, are they perhaps unconsciously suggesting that they do not really want to rebel, that an image of doing so may be enough, and that the real thing might be too dangerous, psychologically speaking? In addition, how can they identify with a hero who holds no hope of ever having any real sexual gratification? Is it possible that Max Headroom's humor and his comic persona are a form of sublimation?

There is also something bizarre about a character talking to and interacting with his electronic alter ego, or is it his own alter image? This image is independent of Carter yet created out of him, by a boy, no less, who is handy with a computer. Does the power to use computers and create images have a sexual dimension? Do many young people identify with Bryce, who seems to find considerable pleasure fiddling at his keyboard?

Another reason young people (and others as well) may find Max Headroom so appealing is that he represents a dream (and hope) for immortality that many people find attractive. Futurists talk about being able, in the not-too-distant future, to transfer the mind, psyche, and personality of individuals (what we might describe as human software) from people's bodies to electronic chips or some other form of hardware, which would mean that people would achieve a kind of eternal life. It is thought, for example, that the astronauts we send to Mars will be robots with the minds of humans embedded on chips or some other electronic devices.

Thus, though we may not admit such things to consciousness, there is an element to the existence of Max Headroom that we find comforting. To adolescents, many of whom feel a great deal of anxiety about the reality of death, Max Headroom represents an answer to their prayers.

Bodies wear out; but electronic devices are easy to manufacture and replicate. In the series, interestingly enough, there are body banks where human parts can be obtained for various purposes—which is only a feeble step in the right direction for those anxious about their mortality. There was an episode, as a matter of fact, in which a young woman was going to be sacrificed in a ghoulish experiment to give an older woman, (who could afford to buy the live body and the experiment) youth and life. Presumably, this kind of thing would not be necessary were Bryce to develop a software program to transfer anyone's mind and personality from their bodies to electronic circuits. This particular episode is a variation of the Frankenstein story, involving the matter of debased science trying to fathom the secrets of life and death and prying into realms that should be, it is suggested, closed to human beings.

The Nightmare Society

Max Headroom takes place in a futuristic nightmare society and recalls the dystopian societies found in films such as *Mad Max*, though it is not quite as extreme and does not posit a nuclear holocaust and wasteland. The series recalls the brilliant MacIntosh commercial "1984." It portrays a world dominated by the mass media and, in particular, television. It is highly stratified, with a small elite controlling the media and the militia and using the media to brainwash everyone and maintain its dominance.

In *Max Headroom*, the situation is not quite as extreme as in "1984," but television does play a major role in the series: it keeps the masses occupied and prevents social chaos. This means that any cessation of television for an extended period of time is a threat to the society, which is posited as existing just at the edge of anarchy. In the series, all the dangers implicit in the information society and the hyper-technology of the modern age are realized. People are under continual supervision (literally), the media are omnipresent (and, by implication, somewhat omnipotent), and there is a counterculture or counterelite of hackers and other mad geniuses who continually threaten the equilibrium of society.

The elites, who control television and society, are self-centered and venal. Political figures are grotesques, who seek only power and money. As represented by the board that governs Channel 23 and employs Edison Carter (and is home to Max Headroom), most of the elites are interested only in ratings—and thus profits and their own well being.

The program makes a powerful statement, then, about what happens in a society when the middle class is destroyed, when society ends up split between a self-serving elite and a depraved mass of others who are essentially powerless and who tolerate (or do not destroy) the status quo because they are kept entertained and distracted. The fact that the program is described as taking place only "twenty minutes into the future" suggest that the creators of *Max Headroom* are alarmed by what they see in society and pessimistic about the future.

This program originated in Great Britain, I might point out, and I understand that what we see is a blander and less biting satire on British society and politics than the British program. In Britain, where class differences are much more powerful and the impact of class differences are more profound, it would be natural to expect the program to be much sharper in its criticisms. *All in the Family* was a much milder portrayal of bigotry and class conflict than the original *Till Death Us Do Part* for the same reasons. In America, we do not have the same rigid class differences, and the barriers to membership in the various elites are not as strong—or at least do not seem to be as strong.

Peter Wagg, who developed the series, said that he has been pleased by the cooperation he's got from the American Broadcasting Company, the network that is airing the program. In an article by Kathryn Baker, "Make Room For a New Cult Hero," Wagg says, "They have really been very supportive and never tried to dilute or take any of the edge off the series." (1987, 3) One reason for this may be that since the show is science fiction and projected into the future, its political significance is not a big issue. For most people who watch it, the show is pure entertainment and its political and social satire isn't an important consideration.

The fact that ideological considerations are not blatant and that the show isn't obviously pitching a political message is one of its strengths. One problem with mixing political ideology and the arts is that the ideology overwhelms everything else. Thus, the creators of *Max Headroom* have done a superb job of creating an entertainment that is primarily an exciting show, but which also has important things to say about society and politics.

The Grotesques

There are two kinds of grotesques in *Max Headroom*: the visual ones and the moral ones. The visual ones are the punks and maniacs who look strange and who often are strange. But one of the heroes in the series is a punk, so we learn that we cannot always evaluate people by the way they look. Far worse, and complicating things endlessly, are the moral grotesques—those who look perfectly normal in their business suits and other ordinary attire, but who are generally both amoral and immoral.

They are the people who are only interested in power and the well-being (or profits) of their organizations. They are careerists who lack moral scruples and evidence little concern with the well-being of the general public. In the opening program, for instance, the members of the board of directors do not decide to take off the blipverts until they were forced to, though, to be fair, there were some members who thought it was bad policy to use them.

The situation is exacerbated by the fact that the masses are portrayed as debased—a vast lumpenproletariat that seethes with discontent but that can be mollified by television. In this situation, though the elites control the masses, they are in a sense captives of them and must continually find new sensations for their television programs to keep the masses quiet.

This is a satire on the situation in America, where television stations compete with one another for viewers and ratings, which generate revenues from advertising. In America, television is a particularly powerful force, and the characters on *Max Headroom* who run Channel 23 are, one might argue, not that far removed from the ones found in the real television networks. It might seem that the show is biting the hand that feeds it, but in the logic of *Max Headroom*, the American Broadcasting Company is primarily interested in profits, and if by presenting a program that ridicules the television industry it can make profits, *that* is what is crucial. The situation with the network, then, parallels the situation posited by the program, in which it is audience numbers that are crucial.

In this ambience of tension, in which the ratings are posted every second, Max Headroom appears and disappears at his own volition and clowns around, mocking the powerful and exposing their villainy. He is their Frankenstein, a creature that escaped from his creator and who wreaks havoc on their world, though Max is funny and a positive figure.

Producing

The film director whose work comes to mind when you watch *Max Headroom* is Ridley Scott. He directed *Blade Runner* and the MacIntosh "1984" commercial. You find his grainy style and the futuristic and surrealistic landscapes he likes, as well as imaginative and interesting camera shots and cutting. Technically, the program is superbly done and the acting is uniformly first-rate. The dialogue is very literate, and Max Headroom's sarcastic remarks and humorous comments are often piquant.

Max Headroom looks like it costs a lot to produce. According to the producer, Peter Wagg, "What we're really doing is making feature films on television . . . the scope of imagination and the look of it and the production values are much more rooted in feature films than television." (1987, 3) Since it is not unusual for a run-of-the-mill television action-adventure program to cost a million dollars for an hour, it is likely that *Max Headroom* costs a good deal more than that. The program represents a considerable investment, then, which ABC hopes to make up for by attracting a large audience for the first showings and later on for the inevitable reruns.

Why the British?

Consider that the two most interesting social and political satires in recent years, *All in the Family* and *Max Headroom*, originated in Great Britain. I might also add *The Prisoner*, another show with political significance, to this trio, which is also from Britain. (*The Prisoner*, a fascinating series done in the sixties, involves a secret agent who is kidnapped and placed on an island where those in control continually try to find out what he knows and use every technique they can to get the information they want. The series does not have the technical qualities that *Max Headroom* has, but it is a fascinating parable about the struggles an individual has in a totalitarian society and the ability of a resolute individual to triumph.)

I imagine that it is the seeming classlessness of American society and its openness that somehow inhibits the creation of biting political television satires. Our society might not produce as many "angry young men" who are full of ideological zeal as Britain does.

In an era of Watergate, Iran-Contra, and Bork hearings, with radio and television full of incredible events and bizarre characters at high levels of government, political satire may not be necessary. It may have been pre-empted by reality. It may be that we don't need Edison Carters since we have reporters who are doing the same thing, except that we are dealing with reality and not fantasy. And our reality is more fantastic and incredible than anything any writer for *Max Headroom* could dream up.

It may also be that we reserve our serious work for film and the theatre. Television attracts an enormous audience and the people who direct it may have anxieties about offending viewers—or boring them. The existence of *Max Headroom* suggests that at least one television network was willing to take a chance with something different; it may also be that as the networks lose audiences (and they have been losing them to cable and videocassette viewing) they are being forced to gamble a bit, to produce shows that may lure people back to the television screen.

The existence of a program such as *Max Headroom* shows that there is nothing in the medium of television that prevents directors and producers from creating superb shows. It is the economic system of television, which *Max Headroom* so brilliantly satirizes, that has turned the medium into the "cultural wasteland" that it is. (A wit has said that "radio is the theatre of the mind and television is the theatre of the mindless.") And the brief existence of the series—it was killed after a summer season and just half a dozen fall episodes were shown—suggests that the economics of television may have a fatal stranglehold on programming. Those who want to experiment and make creative and intelligent programs might be working in the wrong medium.

Max Headroom is Coopted

Max Headroom, as anyone who watches much television knows, has had an ironic fate. He has been coopted by the Coca-Cola company, and instead of mocking the greedy and ridiculing the powerful,

Max now is used to peddle Coca-Cola in commercials to the millions of youngsters (and others) who presumably find him so wonderfully attractive.

On the other hand, Gary Trudeau has parodied the show and created the character Ron Headrest, to poke fun at Ronald Reagan, which shows that this talking head has become an important part of our popular culture and has transcended his origin. He is now a pop icon, a figure that we all recognize and one which (or is it who?) can be used for many purposes. Quite likely Max would find some of the purposes to which he is being put (and will be put) not to his liking; on the other hand, others would amuse him no end.

Unfortunately, since his cancellation, he will amuse us no more—an ironic fate for a character who satirized the very forces that led to his termination.

The ultimate control is, in fact, the view we hold of social reality and our understanding of our own and other people's place within it, including our resistance to the actions and beliefs of others we dislike and repudiate. Life consists essentially of constantly negotiating our understanding with other people, establishing and maintaining by social controls and resistances our own virtue and those of our kind (although in their case not quite as much!) and the immorality and irrationality of others.

It can be suggested that humor plays a fundamental role in these negotiations. As such it can be seen as the baseline of social control, an initial defining mechanism which clarifies and differentiates for the users the "normal" from the "abnormal" or socially deviant.

—*Chris Powell*, Humor in Society: Resistance and Control.

7

Humor and the Jews

Definitional Problems with Humor

It is always difficult to deal with humor because it has a kind of ineffable quality about it. We know what humor is when we experience it; indeed, in some respects humor is an involuntary response to certain kinds of stimulation. But what humor is and why we laugh has challenged the greatest minds throughout history—Aristotle, Kant, Hobbes, Bergson, and Freud, to name just a few. The number of philosophers, psychologists, and other thinkers who have tried to make sense of humor is enormous and so is the literature on humor. We have everything from philosophical speculations to research reports by psychologists, from learned treatises to "how to be funny" books.

There is a good reason for all this interest. People always seek humor because we seem to need it. Humor is a kind of ineluctable force that deals with every aspect of our lives with little concern for propriety or politics. Nothing is sacred to the humorist, and anything and everything is grist for the militancy of some humorist. In this chapter I will discuss various theories of humor and then deal with the unique role humor plays in Jewish culture and society.

Theories of Humor

There are a number of commonly held theories of humor that attempt to explain why it is that people laugh. What follows is a brief overview of the basic theories of humor: the superiority theory, the psychoanalytic theory, the incongruity theory, and what might be called the cognitive theory. There are many other theories, but these seem to be the dominant ones.

The Superiority Theory

The greatest or most important exponents of superiority theories of humor are Aristotle and Hobbes. Aristotle argued that comedy is based upon "an imitation of men worse than average" and Hobbes said that

> the passion of laughter is nothing else but sudden glory arising from some sudden conception of some eminency in ourselves by comparison with the infirmity of others, or with our own formerly. (Hobbes, 1957)

Thus, humor arises out of a sense of superiority relative to others or to the way we once were. This sense of glory must be "sudden" and has an element of strong feelings, "passion," to it.

If we see a man slip on a banana peel, then, we laugh because we feel superior to him and all humor is based on feelings of the same kind. We always feel superior to those we laugh at and when we laugh at ourselves, we feel superior to the way we once were.

Humor reflects, then, some kind of hierarchical arrangement or system of differentiation that exists between ourselves and others or between ourselves and the way we once were.

The Psychoanalytic Theory

This theory was made famous by Freud, who wrote a classic book on the subject, *Jokes and Their Relation to the Unconscious*. One of the basic elements of this theory involves the notion that humor is based on masked aggression. Freud elaborated a very complicated theory, but it would seem that there is a great deal of hidden hostility in humor in which id impulses camouflage aggressive feelings and thus evade constraints that ordinarily would be generated by the superego.

As Freud wrote in *Jokes and Their Relation to the Unconscious*:

> And here we can understand what it is that jokes achieve in the service of their purpose. They make possible the satisfactions of an instinct (whether lustful or hostile) in the face of an obstacle that stands in its way. (1963, 100–101)

The obstacle, of course, is good taste, manners, conscience, or the superego.

All of this is unconscious and the humorist is not aware of what is being done. (It might be argued that the hostile message is transmitted from the unconscious of the humorist to the unconscious of the person who laughs without either party being aware of the full dimensions of the communication.) If you listen carefully to the monologues by Johnny Carson or to any other comedian, you will find a great deal of aggression, insult and hostility which is made acceptable by the presence of humor.

A joke that falls flat does so, it might be argued, because the hostile nature of the joke is not adequately hidden by the humor. There are numerous other aspects of humor that Freud discusses, involving such matters as sexuality and the way the mind functions, but masked aggression is probably the key element in his theory.

His book also has a lot of wonderful jokes in it.

From the psychoanalytic perspective, the man who slips on the banana peel is seen as funny because the submerged hostile and aggressive feelings we have towards others are accidentally satisfied without our being involved, which involves an economy in the expenditure of feelings.

Incongruity Theories

The basic notion in incongruity theories is that there is a difference between what we are led to expect and what we get and that this incongruity is the most common element of all humor. Kant, one of the foremost incongruity theorists, suggested that "laughter is an affectation from the sudden transformation of a strained expectation into nothing."

Thus there is always some kind of a contrast or opposition involved in incongruity theories. (Bergson talked about humor involving "something mechanical being encrusted upon the living" and there are numerous variations on that theme.) In the case of the man slipping on a banana peel, the difference between what we expect (that he will continue on walking) and what we get (his sudden slipping) generates the laughter.

Jokes, which can be defined as "narratives with a punch line" are good examples of incongruity in action. It is the punch line in jokes, the line which offers some kind of a surprising resolution to a situation, that generates the humor. But jokes, we must remember, are not the only form of humor. They are an important form of humor, because they are easy to tell and seem to arise ''spontaneously'' out of the collective consciousness of any society, but we must not confuse jokes and humor.

Cognitive Theories of Humor

The basic interest of cognitive theorists is how we make sense of things, how our minds work and the way paradox informs much of humor. Cognitive theorists see humor as a kind of information that we process and are interested in what special qualities this information has that generates laughter and humor.

One of the most interesting of the cognitive theories involves semiotics, the science of signs. Semiotics is concerned with signification and how we find meaning in things; one of the most important of the semioticians, Lévi-Strauss, has elaborated a methodology called structuralism, which focuses upon the elements in a text and how they are related to one another. Humor is obviously connected to meaning, and since much of humor involves narrative texts, structuralism can be used to analyze these texts and see what they are really about.

For the semiotician, the man who slips on a banana peel involves such matters as the banana peel as a sign (which experience tells us is ''dangerous'') and the opposition between the man walking and the man slipping, the man as a dignified being (before he slips) and the man as a kind of fool or clown (when he slips), between the vertical and the horizontal, and so on. One of the cardinal principles of semiotics is that meaning arises out of the opposition of concepts; thus all humor involves oppositions which can be elicited and which play an important role in the generation and comprehension of humor.

Humor Studies in This Country

Humor has become a major aspect of the American entertainment industry. In recent years comedy clubs have mushroomed all over America, and it is estimated that rather ordinary comedians can make a decent living on the comedy club circuit. Comedians lead comedy workshops at corporations (to teach people how to relax, be more creative, etc.) and there are organizations that conduct comedy workshops all over America.

There is also a great deal of interest in humor in the universities. There are now annual conferences on humor in America and there are international conferences on the subject every other year, as well. There is even an international conference on Jewish humor that alternates between America and Israel.

The enormous popularity (and profitability) of *The Cosby Show* on television has given the situation comedy a great boost and television is now creating numerous situation comedies to ride the wave of popularity of this genre.

And recently, *Humor*, a new journal (with refereed articles, no less) about the subject, has come into being, published by Mouton. Humor is a vital force in this country: its power and popularity are great but why we laugh still remains an enigma.

The Enigma of the Jews

It is obvious that humor is a puzzle to us. The same can be said about the Jews. There is considerable debate about what Jews are. Are they a people, a culture, an ethnic group, a religion, a tribe—or something else? Jews have a basic set of religious principles and the Torah (which is why they are sometimes described as the "people of the book") but can one make any other useful generalizations about them?

We know that there are all kinds of people from all races and ethnic groupings who are Jews. If one's mother was Jewish, one is Jewish, according to principles accepted by most Jews. The logic behind this is quite simple: one always knows who the mother of a child is; one never can be certain about who the father is.

What is significant for our purposes is that Jews traditionally have a well-developed sense of humor, and they use humor for a variety of purposes. In the United States, an unusually high percentage of comedians and humorists are Jews, although this is not unusual, since an unusually high percentage of almost any group (whether it be cult members or Nobel laureates) is Jewish.

A Crazy Hypothesis about Jews and Humor

In the Torah (the first five books of the Old Testament) there is a famous story about Abraham and Sarah. When she was a very old lady (ninety) God told him that she would bear a son, from whom the Jewish people would spring:

And God said to Abraham, "As for your wife Sarai, you shall not call her Sarai, but her name shall be Sarah. I will bless her; indeed, I will give you a son by her. I will bless her so that she shall give rise to nations; rulers of peoples shall issue from her." Abraham threw himself on his face and laughed, as he said to himself, "Can a child be born to a man a hundred years old, or can Sarah bear a child at ninety?" (Genesis, 17:15)

God commanded Abraham to name this son Isaac, which means "laughter" in Hebrew.

Later on in the story Sarah overhears God telling Abraham that Sarah will bear a son and she laughs to herself. When God asks her about this she lies and says she didn't laugh, but she cannot fool God, who tells her that he knows that she did.

When Isaac is born, Sarah says "God has brought me laughter; everyone who hears will laugh with me." There is something significant about having the person from whom all the Jews sprung named "laughter." In addition, there is a famous story about God "testing" Abraham by ordering him to sacrifice Isaac. There are many complexities to this story but for our purposes we can see it as a metaphor involving the preservation of laughter amongst the Jews.

Just when Abraham is about to kill "laughter" an Angel of God tells him not to do so, and instead Abraham kills a ram (the first "stand in") which he sees caught in the woods. Read this way, laughter is to remain a fundamental aspect of the Jewish personality and is, indeed, the source from which Jews spring.

Pilpul

There is something else in the Jewish experience that is relevant here, and that is the fact that Jews have always been literate. The Bar Mitzvah ritual involves having young Jewish males read to the congregation, and it often involves having them offer a critical analysis of some passage or story from the Torah.

In the shtetls of Eastern Europe and among Orthodox Jews today, who are trained in yeshivas, Jewish houses of learning, there is a practice that also has important implications relative to humor, a phenomenon known as pilpul. This has been described by Sborowski and Herzog in *Life is with People* as follows:

Talmudic study is often called *pilpul*, meaning pepper, and it is as sharp, as spicy, as stimulating as its name implies. It involves comparisons of different interpretations, analysis of all possible and impossible aspects of the given problem, and—through an ingenious intellectual combination— the final solution of an apparently insoluble problem.

Penetration, scholarship, imagination, memory, logic, wit, subtlety—all are called into play for solving a talmudic question. The ideal solution is the *khiddush*, an original synthesis that has never before been offered. The mental activity is a delight both to the performer and his audience. Both enjoy the vigor of the exercise and the adroitness of the accomplishment. (1952, 98)

There is good reason to believe that people who are trained in pilpul (and perhaps those who are brought up in a culture where this kind of thing is in the cultural environment, even if in a diluted form) would have the kind of minds that we find in humorists. If you secularize pilpul you get, instead of Torah scholars, comedians.

In an article called "Jewish Jokes and Their Relation to Masochism," which appeared in Werner Mendel's *A Celebration of Laughter*, Martin Grotjahm (who is not Jewish) writes:

There is not a Jewish unconscious, as there is not a Jewish brain or a Jewish cancer. In the strictest sense of the word, there also is not a Jewish character type. There are perhaps certain trends in the Jewish person which develop as his specific way of adjustment to his environment, his idea of being Jewish, his tradition and identity. There is something we call "Jewish wit," which is significant for an adjustment of the Jewish personality, and born out of the needs of his unconscious, trained by his early infantile upbringing, and grown in response to his environment. There are some specific features in the Jewish education, the Jewish background and environment, which may perhaps help to explain some character trends which we often assign to the Jewish persons. (1970, 141)

Grotjahn suggests that Jewish mothers play a central role in socializing their children and mentions the fact that Jews are seen by others as members of a minority, a matter that I believe is of central importance and which I discuss below.

The Social Marginality of the Jews

Although the Jewish presence is very strong in this country (and in world history), we must remember that the Jews have always been a minority and often a relatively powerless one. In a world with something like four billion people, there are only twelve million Jews. In

America, Jews make up but 3 percent of the population. It is sometimes hard for Jews in America to recognize that 97 percent of the people are not Jewish or for non-Jews to realize that only three of every hundred Americans are Jewish.

In a condition of social marginality and political weakness, Jews have to find ways of safeguarding their rights and of dealing with feelings of aggression or hostility. Their use of humor makes good sense then; it can be used to focus criticism (without seeming to do so) on social and political matters and it also allows hostile and aggressive feelings to be expressed without penalty.

Judaism is also a moral force and this tradition, of seeking justice and doing what is right, informs much humor for the Jews. Jewish humor is an egalitarian force, seeking to protect the rights of a small and relatively weak minority by insisting on justice for all and subtly reminding people of their moral obligations to one another.

In a paper titled "The Impact of Mirth and Humor," William Fry, a psychiatrist who has conducted much important research on humor, discusses its social and political impact. He writes:

> Humor is more than a passive stereoscope through which to visualize the culture's ego and behavior. By contributing to the possibilities for self-appraisal, humor encourages the development of self-corrective measures within a social group.
>
> Alterations of social structure and direction are brought about by humor in another, more subtle fashion. This mechanism operates by virtue of the emotional cathartic effects associated with experiencing mirth. These effects cause a trending of the spirit of the culture, through their influence of augmenting, or diminishing, other emotions. Humor influences—such as increasing the atmosphere of acceptance—can be far more effective in the actual life experiences of members of a culture than political exhortation or budgetary statistics, etc. (Fry, 1975)

From this perspective, humor is a tool that has forced the Jews to keep in touch with societal trends and has helped the Jews survive—emotionally as well as politically.

The Problem of Masochism

It was Freud (a Jew) who suggested that no people make more fun of themselves than the Jews. The fact that he used the word "fun" is important, for it suggests that Jewish humor, which often is self-deprecating, is far from being masochistic. One might argue that it is just the opposite.

Grotjahn, in the "Jewish Jokes" essay cited above, argues that the Jewish joke only seems to be masochistic. He writes:

> According to Sigmund Freud and Theodor Reik, no other people on earth, in the past or the present time, has taken itself so mercilessly as the butt of its own jokes as the Jewish people. It is as if the Jewish joke in sophisticated refinement shows the cruel enemy how to be hostile and still remain human. The Jewish joke, however, is only a masochistic mask; it is by no means a sign of masochistic perversion. The Jewish joke constitutes victory by defeat. The persecuted Jew who makes himself the butt of the joke deflects his dangerous hostility away from the persecutors onto himself. The result is not defeat or surrender, but victory and greatness. (1970, 137)

The humor of the Jews, Grotjahn adds, suggests that the Jews preempt their critics by showing that they know their weaknesses and can make fun of them. It is the political weakness, one might add, that makes self-deprecating humor a rational ploy.

There is also an element of superiority to be found, hidden in the background, here. The Jews, who make fun of themselves, often do so from a feeling (generally masked) of moral and intellectual superiority, which makes the pose of self-criticism and the seeming masochism of many Jewish jokes all the more delicious. There is also an element of joy and pleasure to all of this which we should keep in mind, for humor creates pleasure and delight.

We must also remember that not all Jewish humor is pseudo-masochistic or self-deprecating, or deals with the relations between Jews and non-Jews.

There are, I would suggest, two kinds of Jewish humor. The first stems from the old world and is the humor of the shtetl, the humor of Chelm (a town of fools), the humor we often find in collections of Jewish folktales. This humor is peopled with all kinds of characters such as shlemiels (people who are accident prone and are always spilling soup on people) and schlimazels (people who are the victims of accidents and are always having soup spilled upon them), schnorrers (panhandlers), schadkens (marriage brokers), shmegeges, schmendricks, shnooks, luft mensch, rabbis, etc.

Old World and New World Jewish Humor

There is a kind of warmth and humanity in this humor and an acceptance of human frailty. That explains why all the various bizarre character types survive (even flourish) in this shtetl, for though the Jews there were hemmed in by hostile forces, within the shtetl itself there was an element of openness and tolerance, of love and of warmth. The rabbi was the central figure in the communities of the old world and, as might be expected, many of the stories in old world Jewish humor deal with rabbis. Here is a classic story from what I call old world Jewish humor.

> A woman comes to a rabbi and starts telling him about all the terrible things her husband has done. As she goes through her list, the rabbi nods his head and says, "you're right, you're right." She leaves and shortly afterwards the woman's husband comes, and gives his side of the story. He recites a long list of terrible things his wife has done. As he talks, the rabbi nods his head and says, "you're right, you're right." The man leaves. The rabbi's wife, who has overheard both the wife and her husband, then asks the rabbi, "how can you tell the husband and the wife that each of them is right when they contradict one another about everything?" The rabbi nodded his head and said "you're right, too."

In one sense, the rabbi seems to be somewhat of a fool, who agrees with whomever is complaining to him, but in truth, he is a very wise man who realizes that in certain situations logic is of no use and what people need is a sympathetic ear and a chance to talk about their problems. Thus his wife was correct, from a logical point of view, but the rabbi was correct from an emotional one.

The other kind of humor is what might be called new world humor, the humor of contemporary American society (and other societies as well). This is the humor of Jack Benny, Sid Caesar, Woody Allen, and Jackie Mason, and it centers around the problems Jews face in dealing with their families and loved ones in the context of a much more open (and less religious) society. This is the humor of the Jewish mother jokes, the Jewish American princess jokes, the priest, minister and rabbi jokes, the psychiatrist jokes, and that kind of thing. This humor deals with contemporary individuals and types (many of whom are neurotic), Jewish social problems, Jewish personality, Jewish moralism and ethics, politics, and various other topics.

Here are a couple of the classic Jewish mother jokes.

A mother brings her son two ties for his birthday.
"Thanks, mom," he says, and rushes up to the bedroom to put on one of the ties. When he comes down his mother looks at him and says "What's the matter, you don't like the other tie?"

A Jewish mother is complaining about her son. "Oy," she says, "he's a source of pain and pleasure." "How is he a source of pain?" asks a friend. "He's a homosexual, " replies the mother. "How is he a source of pleasure?" "He's going with a doctor," replies the mother.

In the first joke, we can see that the son is placed in an impossible position and that no matter what he does, it will be "wrong" or misconstrued. By implication, then, the Jewish mother always places her children in situations in which they can never "please" her. In the second joke, we notice that she becomes the central figure in the joke and it is her feelings that are central. Also, her disappointment that her son is a homosexual is lessened by the fact that her son has an alliance with a doctor, the figure with the highest status in the Jewish pantheon, because of his professional status and earning power.

Jewish minority status and marginality also explain, I would argue, the passion of Jews for professions. For many years, even in America, which prides itself on being a land of opportunity, positions in banks and universities and numerous other large institutions were not available due to antisemitism, which meant that Jews had to find professions in which they could set up in business (literally and figuratively) for themselves. In addition, the Jewish historical experience of suffering pogroms and expulsions makes having a profession or skill that one can carry with one extremely valuable.

In the same light, the blocked mobility of the Jews led a number of them to become comedians and entertainers. In addition, there might also have been a need to be admired and accepted by the general population as a motivating force. Humor becomes a means of reversing things. One moves from being a member of a "despised race," as some have characterized the Jews, who would want to hide from public view, to occupying center stage and through humor gaining personal acceptance, and, not incidentally, great financial rewards. Jews were not kept out of the entertainment world, which is why so many Jews (relatively speaking) are in that area.

At the same time, through humor, the Jewish comedian could deal with social and political matters and, in subtle ways, help shape public opinion. Humor has, it is generally held, therapeutic significance, so

Jews, as people of "the book" and as moralists and healers, would naturally be drawn to it. Jews are not only overrepresented in comedy but also in therapeutic fields. A lawyer is often defined (in Jewish humor) as "a Jew who can't stand the sight of blood," but one could use therapist or social worker in the joke as well.

The Jewish American Mother and the Jewish American Princess

We have already discussed the Jewish American mother and said something about the problems she poses for Jewish American males. There is a famous joke about a Jewish mother who, upon hearing that her son is going to a psychiatrist and paying him $100 an hour to help the son deal with his Oedipus problem, says "Oedipus, Shmoedipus— as long as he loves his mother." This joke alludes to the "psychic carnage" the Jewish mother is supposed to inflict upon her son, and, by extension, her children. The stereotypes of the Jewish American mother are that she is too solicitous about her children: she forces food on her children, wants her daughters to marry professional men, loves the role of the martyr, controls through guilt, and demands unending love and attention.

It is the Jewish mother who (like most mothers) has primary responsibility for socializing her children, and thus is implicitly responsible for the notorious Jewish American princess (JAP). Her characteristics are reflected in the following jokes.

Antipathy to cooking and sex

What is the JAP's favorite design for a house?
6,000 square feet, without a kitchen or bedroom.

How do you keep a JAP from screwing?
Marry her.

Materialism

How does a JAP commit suicide?
Piles her clothes on the top of the bed and jumps off.

These jokes are generally told by men and reflect strong feelings of hostility and animosity, somewhat disguised by humor, about Jewish women.

In one sense, the Jewish men have accepted the stereotype of Jewish materialism found in jokes about Jews, internalized it, and redirected it against Jewish women. That way, the men escape the negative aspects of this stereotype by directing it against a "stand in" figure. "It is true," the men are saying, "but it doesn't apply to us but, instead, to our women." These jokes may also be connected to a kind of time lag, when women didn't work but just "took" what their husbands provided. Nowadays, with a high percentage of women (including Jewish women) working, the situation has changed.

It might also be that Jewish males find it difficult to "attack" or criticize their mothers and so Jewish women and wives provide a useful substitute. Some elements of the Jewish princess jokes are connected to the American experience and the stereotype of American women (in some cases English women, too) as passionless and sexless.

> A man sees a woman drowning at a deserted beach in France. He tries to rescue her but by the time he reaches her, she is dead. He pulls the dead body from the sea, places it on the sand, and goes off looking for help. When he returns he sees a man having intercourse with the dead body. "Good Lord," says the first man, "You are having sex with a dead woman." "Is that it?" replies the second. "I thought she was American."

There may be elements of this stereotype which have been picked up in the Jewish princess jokes. To the extent that Jews have assimilated into American culture, so the logic suggests, their women have lost interest in sex. Stereotypes of Americans also suggest that they are materialistic, so that the materialistic Jewish princess is only reflecting one of the imperatives of her culture. Thus, the cost of Americanization is great.

The Jewish princess, who won't cook and won't eat and won't have sex, is a reversal of the Jewish mother and represents a reaction against her. (The Jewish mother is always cooking and is always feeding people, though her sex life is something of a mystery.) The princess is a rejection of the Jewish mother who, as we know from the light-bulb jokes, is so self-sacrificing that she will sit in the dark rather than trouble her children.

There is an interesting structural similarity, in reverse, found in the "two ties" joke and the relationship of women to the Jewish American male (or, as some put it, the Jewish American prince). Just as the Jewish son cannot wear both ties at the same time, and in choosing one rather than the other generates a problem, so do the two role models of Jewish women, at both poles, cause trouble. Neither are satisfactory and one has to choose one or the other—or opt out and find a non-Jewish wife.

These jokes only seem innocuous. In truth, they generate unhealthy stereotypes and complicate relationships between Jewish men and women, and they attempt to put women down and minimize their achievements. They are ultimately a reflection of the self-hatred felt by many Jews, who (without being conscious of it) accept the negative stereotypes of Jews and apply these stereotypes to Jewish women so that they don't have to apply them to themselves.

Humor about the Jews

Alan Dundes has written a fascinating article dealing with stereo-types about Jews and Polish Americans ("Polaks" in the jokes, an ethnic slur similar to the term "kike" used for Jews). The stereotype of the Poles is that they are stupid; the stereotype of the Jews is that they are materialistic, status crazy, have big noses, are obsessed by Jewishness and the Jewish problem, and are antipathetic to intermarriage.

The jokelore and folklore about ethnic groups is all-pervasive and generally not very kind. (In England, the kind of jokes that are told about Polish people in America are told about the Irish.) At one time this kind of stereotyped humor was more or less laughed off and considered unimportant, but in recent years, in America at least, ethnic humor has become unacceptable on the public airways and in the mass media. Ethnic jokes still flourish in America and no doubt always will, for wherever there are differences among people, there are jokes and there is ridicule. In countries that are unified ethnically, such as Denmark, people from Copenhagen tell jokes about people from Aarhus (since they don't have Poles, Jews, etc. to make fun of, though they do have political refugees from abroad now, which will no doubt change things). There are endless numbers of jokes full of stereotypes of Americans, the English, the French, the Italians, Germans, Russians, and so on, each pursuing his particular passion.

A commission is established to write about elephants. The Germans produce a three-volume work entitled ''A short introduction to the history of the elephant.'' The French produce a volume, ''The love life of the elephant.'' The English produce a volume on ''Elephant hunting in India.'' The Italians write a book, ''Elephants and the Renaissance.'' The Americans do a book ''Breeding bigger and better Elephants.'' And a Jew does a book, ''Elephants and the Jewish question.''

This joke pokes fun at national stereotypes, and it also points out the degree to which the Jews are obsessed about how anything and everything relates to the Jews. Given the situation of Jewish marginality, and the fact of the holocaust, prosemitism and antipathy to intermarriage (which, in principle, would lead to the disappearance of the Jews) can be understood. Humor remains an enigma. It has great power for good (and as the Jewish American princess jokes show, for bad).

Central to understanding Jewish humor is Jewish marginality. As a result of this, Jews seek a just society where they will not be discriminated against, where they will be treated equally. Thus, the ethical foundations of Judaism and the social marginality of the Jews in America (and elsewhere) generate what I would describe as an egalitarian culture and this egalitarianism is reflected in Jewish humor, which criticizes the ''rich, well born and able,'' and suggests that human beings have, ultimately, the same needs and the same rights. From the fact of Jewish marginality in America, everything else follows.

I would also note, in conclusion, that the Blacks are now an important element in the American comedy scene. They too are marginal (being ten percent of the population), they too have grievances, and they too use humor as a means of criticizing social and political matters that cause them problems. There is some humor that comes from superior social groups laughing at those beneath them, but in America (and, I would imagine, in most other places) humor is a form of masked criticism of the hierarchies (political, social, and economic) by those whom I have called egalitarians.

What is portrayed in wrestling is therefore an ideal understanding of things; it is the euphoria of men raised for a while above the constitutive ambiguity of everyday situations and placed before the panoramic view of a univocal Nature, in which signs at last correspond to causes, without obstacle, without evasion, without contradiction. . . In the ring, and even in the depths of their voluntary ignominy, wrestlers remain gods because they are, for a few moments, the key which opens Nature, the pure gesture which separates Good from Evil, and unveils the form of a Justice which is at last intelligible.

—*Roland Barthes*, Mythologies

8

Professional Wrestling

Introduction

Professional wrestling is a curiosity that lingers on the margins of American culture, sustained by our insatiable need for entertainment and waxing and waning in cycles that defy explanation. Sometimes wrestling is "big" and attracts a good deal of interest; at other times, and most of the time, it is small potatoes.

It would be a big mistake to assume, however, that professional wrestling, especially as it is seen on television, is a trivial matter. Just the opposite, as a matter of fact, if you accept my contention that wrestling is the "immoral or amoral equivalent" (for it is certainly not the "moral equivalent") of political science for many men and women in America.

Roland Barthes on Wrestling

The first essay in Roland Barthes' classic study of French culture, *Mythologies*, is devoted to wrestling. It might seem rather bizarre that Barthes, one of France's leading intellectuals and culture critics, would write on this topic. Wrestling seems so trivial, so insignificant in the scheme of things. But Barthes also discussed topics such as soap powders, margarine, toys, steak and chips, the striptease, and plastic—because he felt that these topics enabled him to come to grips with some of the basic mythologies that, to use the Shadow's terminology, were "clouding men's minds."

He analyzed wrestling and these other topics (all examples or part of what we would identify as popular culture) for what they revealed about his society. He believed that wrestling and his other topics played an important role in "mystifying" people, and the purpose of his book was to "demystify" French culture.

One thing that attracted Barthes' attention was the quality of light at the wrestling matches he watched. This light gave the proceedings, he argued, a certain significance. He writes about "the drenching and vertical quality of the flood of light" and says:

> Even hidden in the most squalid Parisian hall, wrestling partakes of the nature of the great solar spectacles, Greek drama and bullfights: in both, a light without shadow generates an emotion without reserve. (1972, 15)

Barthes was a leading practitioner of semiology, the science of signs, and recognized that the lighting of these matches was a kind of sign, one that was found in other spectacles where the quality of the lighting played a facilitating role in the generation of powerful feelings. All television directors are aware of the significance of lighting as a means of establishing different moods in viewers.

Wrestling also is a spectacle of excess, Barthes tells us, and "each sign in wrestling is therefore endowed with an absolute clarity" (1972, 16). It is in the nature of wrestling for the wrestlers, who we might describe as exaggerated personalities (and in many cases, grotesques) to be full of exaggerated gestures. For Barthes, the bodies of wrestlers were important signs, and he spent some time discussing one famous French wrestler, Thauvin, who had a nickname "la barbaque" or "stinking meat." Thauvin, Barthes said, is "a fifty-year-old with an obese and sagging body, whose type of asexual hideousness always inspires feminine nicknames, [and who] displays in his flesh the characters of baseness" (1972, 17). The bodies of wrestlers are signs, then, which people learn to read and interpret on the basis of past experience with other wrestlers, and on the basis of a particular wrestler's past history.

One last point Barthes makes is that wrestling is about public torture and is a "great spectacle of Suffering, Defeat, and Justice. Wrestling presents man's suffering with all the amplification tragic masks" (1972, 19). There is a difference between wrestling in France and America that is important, for according to Barthes, in America wrestling is "a sort of mythological fight between Good and Evil" whereas in France it is different, "being based on ethics and not on politics" (1972, 23). In America, suggests Barthes, the bad wrestler is always supposed to be a Red (Communist) while in France the bad wrestler is a "bastard." One crucial aspect of this bastard role is that of being unpredictable and unstable, accepting rules only when they are convenient. It is this unpredictability that drives audiences wild. "This inconsistency, far more than treachery or cruelty, sends the audience beside itself with rage: offended not in its morality but in its logic, it considers the contradiction of arguments as the basest of crimes" (1972, 24).

I don't think Barthes is correct about everything he says (in particular about bad wrestlers in America) but he does call our attention to the political significance of wrestling and the important matter of "justice" that any analysis of wrestling in America must consider.

Barthes' essay on wrestling is not only an analysis of a significant phenomenon but an important study of theatre, for wrestling is, we can see, a vernacular form of theatre which gives people "the image of passion, not passion itself," which is the essence of the theatrical experience.

Wrestling and the Cult of Personality

College wrestling is a true sport and like all sports involves a certain amount of drama and suspense. But professional wrestling is hard to classify—it is generally described as an "exhibition," a term that doesn't tell us very much. It has sport-like elements in it, in that wrestlers are people with athletic ability and many of them can perform certain moves, know various holds, and that kind of thing. It is supposedly a contest, though there is good reason to believe that the outcome is planned in advance, which suggests that wrestling is, as I have suggested earlier, best described as a kind of vernacular theater.

The most important aspect of this theater are the actors, since the plot is relatively simple, and what a collection of personalities wrestling has created! There are essentially two categories of wrestlers: those who look relatively normal, though they may be very tall or large and powerful men (often very well developed) and the freaks. The freaks are a collection of men who may be extremely fat, or who may be giants, who may affect various ethnic identities and offer diatribes (when they get to the microphone) in various languages, who affect bizarre personalities and who, in one way or another, place themselves out of the mainstream of American culture and society. They are, like Thauvin, "signs" and, like Thauvin, sometimes their flesh has the same kind of asexuality to it that audiences read as repugnant.

Wrestling is full of personalities, one more bizarre than the next. As a result of their hyper-individuality they tend to overwhelm people with a kind of freak-show sensory overload, ultimately minimizing their freakishness. The infinite cultural variety of American society, a society full of immigrants who speak "strange" languages and have "funny" notions, is revealed to the audience. There is a great panorama of stereotypes as mad Russians, cruel Germans, heroic American Indians and Blacks, vicious mid-Easterners, inscrutable Asians parade before us. What is crucial is that the wrestlers visually distinguish themselves in the public's eye.

Weaving their way through this spectacle of excess are the more ordinary looking heroes and villains, who fight one another and the various freaks. The superstar heroes tend to be relatively normal looking and are "charismatic" personalities: they are "fast," know many holds and moves, and generally win their matches.

The Submission Hold

The submission hold represents the element of catastrophe in wrestling, for once a wrestler is able to get this hold on his opponent, victory is inevitable. Matches have become, in essence, contests to see who will be first to be able to use a submission hold—the purest representation of torture in wrestling.

In theory, the submission hold causes so much pain that the person experiencing the hold cannot continue, or the hold "forces" its victim to lose by pinning his back on the canvas for the requisite count of three. There are also so-called sleeper submission holds in which the victim is put to sleep, so his defeat is more or less benign, and he is left sleeping (or knocked out) on the mat.

Wrestlers show great inventiveness in developing the submission holds and derive a certain amount of identity from having a distinctive or unusual one. Some are flamboyant: the wrestler applying the hold might lift his victim up and spin him around before some kind of an acrobatic movement temporarily disables the poor wretch.

The submission hold may be a kind of metaphor for the way many people, especially fatalists who watch wrestling on television, feel about their lives and their relationships with those more powerful, such as bosses, landlords, the police. These victims have been caught, for one reason or another, by some powerful entity and have no choice but to submit and experience some equivalent of being pinned. Watching wrestling, then, becomes a theatrical representation of their lives and they can empathize with the poor wrestlers who become caught in these holds and undergo public humiliation. It is possible, also, that these fatalists fans identify with the winning villainous wrestlers and their questionable values.

Nicknames

Many of the wrestlers have nicknames, especially the heroes and the villains. These nicknames offer added insights into the personalities (or theatrical identities) of the wrestlers. Thus, in the most recent matches I watched on television, there was a wrestler named Adrian "Adorable" Adonis. This name had a double irony, for Adonis was a singularly unpleasant and nasty fellow, and he was also very fat, as far from an Adonis as one can get.

Perhaps the most famous of the American wrestlers was "Gorgeous" George, who may have given the cult of personality and eccentricity in wrestling a major boost. One of the more important contemporary wrestlers is named "Hulk" Hogan, a gigantic blond wrestler who is seen on other kinds of programs, including the Dolly Parton variety show, which suggests that he has become a kind of celebrity and escaped the narrow confines of the wrestling ring.

The Bastard and the Saint

Barthes used the term "bastard" to refer to the villains in wrestling, to legions of "dirty" wrestlers who use any trick (and play upon the stupidity of the referees) for their vile purposes and to win their matches. Usually professional wrestling is a battle between good wrestlers, that is "clean" wrestlers who follow the rules, and "dirty" wrestlers who pay no attention to the rules—except when doing so benefits them.

Dirty wrestlers face two kinds of opponents: sacrificial victims and heroic winners. When the dirty wrestler faces a sacrificial victim, the match becomes a ritual humiliation of the clean wrestler. He may have some moments when he punishes the dirty wrestler, but generally speaking he undergoes a prolonged humiliation and after a sufficient period of being choked, having his eyes gouged, being kicked, thrown into the post, and slammed a number of times, he is dispatched via some submission hold.

In these matches, the clean wrestler is a sacrificial victim who, like a saint, undergoes ordeals and martyrdom, for the sake of his fellow man (and woman). It is no accident that wrestling uses the term "fall," a term with theological connotations. (In Adam's Fall, we sinned all.)

When the bastard wrestles a heroic winner, the situation is more complicated, for here we find the tables are usually turned. Generally speaking, the dirty wrestler uses his devious tricks to punish the hero, but only up to a point. The dirty wrestler must establish himself as a real "bastard" and get the audience excited. The hero, because of his superior strength and resources, turns the tables and punishes the villain—often using the villain's own dirty tricks against him. The wrestling public seems to appreciate this irony.

I have been discussing the two classic forms of wrestling. There are, of course, numerous variations on these two themes, but a large percentage of matches involve the ritual sacrifice of a clean guy to a monstrous villain or the triumph of an heroic "star" wrestler over a villain.

It is obvious that wrestling is very binary in nature and in this black and white world of villains and good guys, there isn't very much room for gray areas. This simplistic world has been described as involving a two-valued orientation, a terribly impoverished perspective on things. Another term used for this mind-set is dichotomous thinking, which is often associated with alienation, ethnocentrism, anomie (normlessness), scapegoating, and a sense that we live in a cruel world.

The political implications of this dichotomous, black and white view of the world are obvious: it implies fatalism and lack of involvement in the political process. To consider that wrestling provides people with a sense of how the world works and has implications for political behavior is disturbing.

Hype

One of the more interesting aspects of televised wrestling is the interviews between announcers and wrestlers. In some wrestling programs, as a matter of fact, wrestlers spend almost as much time at the microphone as they do wrestling. (This is because many of the televised wrestling matches are little more than commercials for forthcoming matches.)

The content of these interviews is standard. Wrestlers insult their opponents, challenge them to "blood" feuds, tell the audiences what they will do to their opponents when they wrestle them, and glorify themselves. The world of wrestling is full of controversies in which wrestlers claim they were "cheated" in some previous match, that their opponents used unfair tactics, and insist that things will be different next time. Different conferences and leagues attack and insult one another also, maintaining turmoil on every level.

It is not unusual for wrestlers with a particular ethnic identity to speak to fans in a foreign language and exhort them to come to some big match. There is a good deal of buffoonery, also. In one television interview, two "Russian" wrestlers showed a picture of Lenin and sang the "Internationale" in Russian as an attack on their opponents and American society in general.

Camp Followers

Wrestling is, obviously, camp—a spoof of itself, lacking seriousness and full of put ons and ploys. What is interesting is that even if those who follow wrestling accept the fact that it is not a real sport, that it is, in other words, fake, it still has an impact on people. And that is because of the willing suspension of disbelief that everyone experiences at theatrical events—and because wrestling often does such a superb job of providing "the image of passion" even if it can't provide the passion itself.

When you see people who seem to be suffering, who are being tortured and enduring gross violations of their humanity, flying around the ring (and being thrown out of it), you cannot help but experience a strong emotion. And when the villains magnify their evil nature by expressions of heartlessness, you can get caught up in things.

When you attend a match, you often feel a sense of electricity in the air. There is excitement and anxiety, even though everyone (or almost everyone) recognizes that they are seeing an "exhibition" and what might be described as "the true theatre of cruelty." Most regular fans of wrestling have learned something about the construction of a typical match, but the execution (and I used the word on purpose) is what is crucial.

What the wrestlers are able to do is both provide a form of theatre that is "camp" and, at the same time, involve audiences emotionally in the matches. Audiences get, then, the best of both worlds: they can claim that the matches are silly and not serious and they can get emotional releases and gratifications as they watch the wrestlers battle (and torture) one another.

"Uses and gratifications theory" tells us that people go to wrestling matches (or watch them on television) because these matches provide certain gratifications that people find important. What uses do people make of wrestling and what gratifications does it provide? Sometimes matches provide audiences with the opportunity to see heroes triumph over villains, reinforcing the notion that we live in a just world. But many matches involve just the opposite, a match between a huge villain and a much smaller good guy who is, so to speak, sacrificed to the villain and undergoes a public ordeal of humiliation and torture. These matches suggest that the world is unfair and that those who follow the rules have little reason to hope for success.

Let me expand on this matter with a discussion of the political implications of the typical match (to the extent that any wrestling match is ever typical).

Political Aspects of Wrestling

In the typical wrestling match we find three characters: a good guy, a villain, and a referee. The referee supposedly has some kind of authority behind him and, for our purposes, may represent the *state* or the *government* in the popular mind. In the match, the good guy follows the rules and the villain doesn't. When the good, *clean* wrestler finds he is forced to adopt the dirty wrestler's tactics, the referee usually ends up preventing the good guy from using these tactics. On the other hand, the villain fights dirty and gets away with it because the referee doesn't see what is going on.

The referee or "state" hinders the good wrestler and unwittingly aids the bad wrestler, and this becomes a metaphor for the way people see government operating. The state, then, is not only powerless to help us but, as it turns out, does more harm than good, for it prevents the hero from defending himself and helps the villain achieve his evil ends. (This is much different from a real sport such as football, where the authority of the referees and umpires is seen as legitimate and is not disputed, though people recognize that sometimes officials make bad calls. This is excused, however, because "people are only human." Fans also assume that the bad and good calls will balance out, so generally speaking no real harm is done.)

In wrestling there is also a kind of anarchy, with different leagues and numerous "world champions." One is reminded of feudalism with its regional rulers and despots—before the development of the all-powerful national state. Wrestling combines, somehow, the gladitorial combats of ancient Rome and the quasi-anarchy of medieval feudal society, and it exists and flourishes in a postmodern society.

Political Messages Found in Wrestling

Evil is Rampant.

The universe of wrestlers is permeated with villains of the grossest nature. We live, wrestling suggests, in a dangerous world, where villains of every conceivable nature abound—villains who will do anything to achieve their ends.

The State is Powerless to Help Us.

In this dangerous world, the state, as symbolized by the referee, cannot help us. It is both too weak and too stupid, unwittingly hindering the heroes and helping the villains. For all practical purposes, then, the state is irrelevant and does not exist as an important entity.

Thus, in a match in which a smaller, clean wrestler was sacrificed to Adrian "Adorable" Adonis (who outweighed his opponent by more than one hundred pounds), Adonis refuse to stop his "sleeper hold" on his opponent even after he had won the match, and the referee was "unable to stop him." The announcer said he feared that the victim might suffer serious injury. He was helped out of the ring, limp, and groggy.

Individuals Must Look Out for Themselves and Get Along as Best They Can.

For many, this involves doing the best you can to survive in an unfair world and undergoing the ordeals and punishment that cannot be avoided as best one can. In an anarchistic society, the weak and powerless survive by adopting a stance that might best be described as *stoicism* or, less kindly, as *fatalism*.

We Must Fight Fire with Fire.

To survive in this cruel and hostile world, we must often adopt the techniques of the villains to get by. Playing by the rules, being moral, and doing the right thing is just an invitation to be ''destroyed.''

The Competition is Unfair.

It is because the state is useless and the villains are more powerful that adopting the tactics of the villains becomes necessary. The villains (and we might read in here ''the rich and powerful'') have an unfair advantage—they have more resources, have numerous advantages, and they fight dirty—so the weaker elements must get by as best they can. In an unjust society, so-called antisocial behavior and crime take on a different meaning and are, ultimately justified, just as the hero is forced to adopt the tactics of the villain and fight dirty in order to win.

There are Conspiracies that Further Exacerbate the Situation.

Without knowing it, the state is often ''a partner to the crime'' since it hinders the hero and helps the villains. It is reasonable to assume that in some cases the state does know what it is doing and conspires with evil elements and villains. Thus, officials are ''paid off'' and the hero only has the illusion that the fight will be honestly refereed. In many cases, the refereeing is irrelevant anyway, since the match is so unfair.

Social Class and Wrestling

The commercials found in wrestling tend to be for fast foods, cars, automotive services, and jewelers for people (as one commercial put it) ''with no credit.'' It seems likely that wrestling appeals to working-class and lower-class people with relatively low educational levels and little discretionary income. Wrestling is carried on local stations and the production qualities are relatively primitive. The primary audience of wrestling must be considerably less demanding than network television viewers.

This audience, with its people who have "no credit," gets a political education from wrestling that is simplistic and destructive. Quite likely the values and world view portrayed in wrestling reinforce the fatalistic, apolitical attitudes that are supposed to be found in the most disadvantaged in society. (I do not believe that many people are conscious of the political education they get from wrestling. It is seen simply as an entertainment, but one in which they see their situation mirrored and which they can understand and empathize with.) To the extent that viewers of wrestling have given up on political participation and adopted a fatalistic (or stoic) stance towards the world, the political education wrestling provides is most unfortunate.

I found in the data of art, literature, philosophy, political and juridical thought, history, comparative religion, and similar documents far more suggestive ideas about the nature of the social than in the work of colleagues doing their "normal social science" under the then prevailing paradigm of structural functionalism. These notions are not always put forward with direct or obvious reference to social relations—often they are metaphorical or allegorical—sometimes they appear in the guise of philosophical concepts or principles, but I see them as arising in the experience of human coactivity. . . . Structure is all that holds people apart, defines their differences, and constrains their actions, including social structure in the British anthropological sense.

    —*Victor Turner,* Dramas, Fields, and Metaphors: Symbolic Action in Human Society

9

The Terminator: A Case Study in High-Tech Paranoia

Introduction

The Terminator is a science fiction film made in 1984 starring Arnold Schwarzenegger as a malevolent cyborg sent from future times to present-day American society to kill a young woman, Sarah Connor. The purpose of this exercise is to prevent her from having children and starting a family whose offspring would exist in the future. In essence, the terminator's job is to change history.

This kind of plot is a common one in science fiction. There was an episode of *Star Trek* in which Spock, Kirk, and McCoy had to let a beautiful young woman be killed in an automobile accident— otherwise history would have been changed with results that would have been disastrous for the world. In this case, the heroes of *Star Trek* were time travelers whose mission was a positive one.

In *The Terminator*, the situation is different. The Terminator is a time-travelling cyborg, a robot with a veneer of flesh, which seems human, that is programmed to accomplish its mission and use whatever means are necessary to do so. A soldier, Kyle Reese, also manages to travel into the past to fight the Terminator, and the film is, in essence, a series of battles between Reese and the Terminator in which Reese attempts to save Sarah Connor from termination.

We know from a flashback of Reese's that terminators exist in the future and see a scene in which a terminator has managed to get into an encampment of freedom fighters. He machine guns people with wild abandon. In that scene, Reese sees a picture of Sarah Connor, the progenitor of a long line of people, which was taken in the distant past.

The Terminator violates one of Asimov's laws for robots—that they will not hurt human beings. It is a nightmare figure, half-machine, half-human (or seemingly human), that stalks Sarah Connor relentlessly and single-mindedly, destroying anyone or anything that interferes with its mission. The Terminator is a Frankenstein monster—it is not human though it approximates human form. But unlike Frankenstein, the Terminator has no feelings.

The Story

In essence, the plot of *The Terminator* is a sustained chase story in which the Terminator, acted with a grim deadness by Schwarzenegger, searches for and attacks Sarah Connor. There are innumerable automobile chases and close escapes. In one scene, Sarah and Kyle are apprehended by the police. A police psychologist interrogates Reese, who tells him about the Terminator in considerable detail. The psychologist concludes that Reese is insane. In one ironic scene, the psychologist is shown leaving the police station just as the Terminator enters, to inquire about Sarah Connor. A short while later, he rams the police station with a car and, machine gun blazing, devastates the station. In the confusion, Reese escapes with Sarah Connor and they race off to a motel far from the city. When Reese goes to a hardware store to purchase some supplies to make bombs, Sarah makes the mistake of calling her mother. She actually talks with the Terminator, who has imitated her mother's voice and who jumps on a motorcycle and sets off for the city and the motel where Sarah and Reese are staying. That night Sarah and Reese make love—and, as it turns out, she is impregnated. The next morning there is a final denouement in which the Terminator, on a motorcycle, dodges bombs made by Kyle Reese. The final scenes, which are terrifying, show the Terminator driving a huge oil rig, all set to run down Sarah. Kyle has put a bomb in the rig and it explodes, turning the truck into a fiery inferno. One would think that would be the end of the Terminator, but such is not the case. The Terminator, stripped of its flesh and revealing itself as a glistening robot, emerges from the blaze and continues to chase after Sarah and Kyle.

The Terminator chases them into a metal factory. Kyle manages to put a bomb on the Terminator, which explodes, killing Kyle and ripping the Terminator in half. The top half of the Terminator, using its arms to crawl, continues to chase Sarah. She runs into a huge press, the Terminator follows, and just before the Terminator can reach her to strangle her, she turns on the press and crunches the Terminator.

At the end, we see Sarah, pregnant, heading towards some mountain in Mexico. When she stops for gas a young Mexican child takes a Polaroid photo of her—the same Polaroid photo we saw in Kyle Reese's flashback.

Thus, the story ends with the Terminator having been foiled and with Sarah Connor pregnant and about to start a line of progeny that will extend far into the future—into the time when many terminators exist, killing people and spreading mayhem.

Psychological Implications

The Terminator reflects a diffuse sense of paranoia that people feel—especially those whom we describe as *fatalists*—who see life as essentially a matter of luck and believe that powerful forces are operating against them. The Terminator is, of course, an extreme example of the power of those who control society, but the ambience of the film, the gritty quality of the parking garages and police stations, is the world of the powerless and fatalistic.

It is only Reese, a warrior with courage and determination, who is able to fight against the Terminator. It wipes everyone else out and seems unstoppable. The relentlessness of the Terminator's behavior is a major source of the terror. It is mindless but it has an intelligence. We see computer readouts on the screen whenever the Terminator comes across a device or situation that needs to be understood. Thus, for example, a computer readout shows it the gearing structure of the oil truck and "teaches" it how to drive it.

Thus, it could be argued that the Terminator is a personification of the sense of despair and oppression fatalists have, a sense that the powers that run society are everywhere and just about all-powerful. (Not completely all-powerful because there has to be room for luck and chance.)

There is also the matter of the anxiety we all feel about machines and, in particular, about machines in the future which may be *intelligent* and may be mobile (that is, robots). Many science fiction stories deal with powerful machines or machinelike creations that have no emotions or feelings and that destroy until they are stopped. One thing that science fiction stories do is raise feelings of anxiety and fear (and sometimes even terror) which they then alleviate by finding ways of destroying the monsters and machines. This gives audiences a sense of well-being and hope.

Let me summarize, then, some of the fatalistic elements reflected in *The Terminator*:

Powerful Forces Attack Us That We Cannot (at Least at First) Deal With.

There Is No Let Up

The Terminator is relentless and even when it is blown up, it still presses forward, trying to accomplish its mission.

One Survives Due to Luck and Chance

It is only such things that enable us to manage, given the nature of the forces that we must contend with.

Authority Is Useless

The police, for example, were both powerless and wrong. Sarah Connor survived in spite of the police, not as the result of their assistance. In fact, they did more harm that good. The moral is—you can't trust the police. When they aren't useless they are harmful.

The Concept of "Termination" Has a Bureaucratic Ring to it

The CIA uses the phrase "termination with extreme prejudice" when they want to have someone killed. "Termination" also suggests that some entity, which has the right and power to do so, decides when to put an end to your employment (or life).

Science Fiction Elements in *The Terminator*

The Terminator is an alien, but not a bug-eyed monster which is easy to detect, even though it may be powerful and scary. What is anxiety provoking about this creature is that it has a human form and thus is not immediately recognizable for what it is. There is also, as I mentioned earlier, the anxiety about intelligent machines and what they might do if, somehow, they become independent or are programmed by some malevolent force.

One interesting aspect of *The Terminator* is its hyper-phallicism. The chosen weapon of the Terminator (and of all terminators, it is suggested in Reese's flashback) is the submachine gun. The substitute phallus of the Terminator is used to kill, not create life. Schwarzenegger, a giant, muscular figure, devastates the police station with his submachine gun. He races from room to room shooting everyone he sees as he searches for Sarah Connor. She has been snatched by Reese, however.

The story also projects a bleak future, for it shows a society in which people who wish to be free are continually being hunted down by submachine gun-toting terminators. Reese's flashback portrays this society.

In a curious way, these stories about alien figures replicate what happens in our bodies when alien force such as germs invade and are attacked. Stories like *The Terminator* are metaphors for infection and disease and replicate the battles that take place in our bodies when alien organisms invade and attempt to destroy them. The AIDS virus is the great "terminator" in present-day society and, as of now, there is no way to deal with this malevolent force. Disease, we may say, is the model for the alien killer, and *The Terminator* and many other science fiction stories are the manifestation of this model. Like the Terminator, these viruses and alien forces seek to kill us, though in so doing, as the biologists point out, they ultimately destroy themselves.

Finally, there is the matter of emotionless intelligence, which is very scary. One of the reasons humans like dogs and other warm-blooded animals is that they have emotion and are animated, responsive creatures. (In *The Terminator*, dogs recognized terminators and barked at them.) Snakes and other reptiles, on the other hand, are single-minded predators and repel us. We fear intelligence without feeling because we all believe that it is our feelings and emotions that humanize us, that temper our reason and prevent us from mindlessly and perhaps destructively following the dictates of our so-called intelligence.

Oppositions in the Text

Lévi-Strauss has suggested that the function of mythic heroes is to mediate between opposing forces and, in some way, reconcile them. Although *The Terminator* is not a myth, it has mythic elements, and in Sarah Connor and the Terminator it has two figures who are very different.

Let me spell out these oppositions below. First, the Terminator is a killer and Sarah Connor is the woman he wants to kill. (All the other killings are incidental, as a matter of fact.) The Terminator is a cyborg, a nonhuman thing, a robot which has a veneer of human flesh around it. Sarah, on the other hand, is a human and a warm and loving one, too. The Terminator chases and attacks, and Sarah and Kyle are chased and attacked. The Terminator is a tall, powerful male and Sarah is a (relatively speaking) weak female—though, as we see at the end, she is a courageous and resourceful one.

The Terminator represents the future which has come into the past and Sarah, through her progeny, represents the past which will extend into the future. She is pregnant with Kyle's child at the end of the film, and we know that her line will play an important role in the future. The Terminator, as its name implies, represents death and is asexual while Sarah represents life and fertility. The Terminator is an alien cyborg (pseudohuman) and Sarah is a "native" human. The Terminator, as a machine, is emotionless. Schwarzenegger does a superb job of capturing this: he is very businesslike. Sarah, on the other hand, is loving and passionate.

The Terminator is self-sufficient while Sarah needs help. Without Kyle she has no chance to survive. It is her survival that is crucial to the story, which, in the final analysis, deals with the central opposition of the story—termination versus continuance. Her survival is the result of Kyle's heroism and sacrifice, terms that would be meaningless to cyborgs. Though Kyle dies, he lives on through the child that he has fathered.

These oppositions, which provide the central meaning of the text, can be seen in the lists below:

The Terminator	The Girl
Cyborg	Human
Killer	Victim
Chases	Is chased

The Terminator	The Girl
Male	Female
The future in the past	The past in the future
Death	Birth
Asexual	Sexual
Evil	Good
Emotionless	Emotional, loving
Self-sufficient	Needs help
Goal: termination	Goal: continuance
Is destroyed	Survives

It is these oppositions that are central to the text and that provide its meaning. And it is the oppressiveness of the film, its portrayal of a powerful alien creature that has but one goal, which it pursues relentlessly, which leads me to suggest that it is a work best described as fatalistic.

The film has a seamy quality, it is full of car chases, with parking garages, police stations, cheap motels, and factories for settings. And worst of all, I would say, is the figure of the Terminator, a perverted superego figure.

A Psychoanalytic Perspective on *The Terminator*

From a psychoanalytic point of view, the Terminator reflects a superego that has become distorted and destructive and is out of control. Sarah is an id (desire, sexuality, impulse) figure in the most positive sense of the term, for as the Freudians tell us, we all need the id which provides energy and, ultimately, life itself. Kyle Reese takes over the role of the ego (reason, survival), trying to mediate between the superego (guilt, conscience) and the id, but because the superego in this case is perverted and obsessive, he cannot use reason or logic but must fight it with its own weapons.

Many years ago, psychiatrists were called "alienists," for it was felt that disturbed or crazy people were, in a sense, aliens or even alienated. The plot of *The Terminator* can be seen as an externalization of the battles that go on, so the Freudians believe, in our psyches between our superegos, our ids and our egos. When one element of the psyche is too powerful and our psyches are out of balance, so the theory goes, we find neuroses and other problems. One reason the film is so disturbing, I would argue, is because it reflects, in vague and disguised ways, a kind of unbalanced collective psyche, in which guilt and related matters have overwhelmed the id (our source of energy) and rendered it ineffective.

This may explain the reliance on luck and the sense of powerlessness that are associated with fatalist political cultures. The id elements are too weak and the ego is rendered ineffective by a distorted superego. *The Terminator* can be seen, from the psychoanalytic perspective, as a little morality drama in which a monstrous superego is destroyed by a valiant ego so that the id can survive.

None of this, I believe, is apparent to the typical viewer of the film. It is just another science-fiction film dealing with a killer alien and full of action and violence. What the psychoanalytic perspective does is offer us a sense of why the film has such a nightmarish quality about it, why it is so disturbing. What I have suggested, also, is that our understanding of people who would be categorized by Wildavsky as fatalists may be enlarged by speculating about the psychoanalytic reasons for their present-mindedness and reliance on luck and chance.

The Terminator was described in one review as having a "comic book" quality about it. I thought the acting was good, and the narrative certainly had a lot of action. *The Terminator* may not be a great work of art, but it is a film that reveals many things about American political culture and society.

Part Two

COMMUNICATION THEORY

By far the most powerful fieldwork methods in the social sciences are those of the structural anthropologists. Undeterred by gaps or apparent contradictions in chronology, able to accommodate dreams and fables, considering variants of the same story as clues to meaning, structural anthropologists take seriously the task of discovering the inner coherence of a way of life. Episodes are compared whenever they occur or however they appear, on the assumption that what matters most to people is how they ought to behave toward one another and how these values are to be embodied in their social practices.

The traditional rabbinic interpreters of the Bible, with centuries of practice, also sought to uncover layers of meaning by comparing biblical episodes. Perhaps it is not surprising, then, that the methods of structural anthropology turn out to be almost a carbon copy of the rules of rabbinic interpretation as these have been handed down in the last two thousand years.

—*Aaron Wildavsky,* The Nursing Father: Moses as a Political Leader

10

The Politics of the Sign:
On the Semiotics of Power

In this book I have used Aaron Wildavsky's adaptation of Mary Douglas's seminal ideas on the four political cultures found in all societies of size and complexity to deal with the political content of American poplar culture, and, in particular, a number of texts that I found to be particularly interesting. I chose two texts for each of Wildavsky's four political cultures. Each text clearly exemplifies, I suggest, the political values associated with one of Wildavsky's four political cultures: hierarchical elitism, egalitarianism, competitive individualism and fatalism.

I have treated each text and the logical audiences for each text as ideal types, even though I realize (and have pointed out earlier) that texts are polysemic—full of different kinds of signs and meanings— and audiences for texts often misread them and their content. I have assumed, for argument's sake, a *good text* that exemplifies one of the four political cultures and a *good reader* who sees in the texts the political values and beliefs that are most directly connected to his or her political culture.

On the Politics of Entertainment

For some people, the notion that entertainments have a political dimension or content (and other dimensions as well) is difficult to accept. I recently was talking with a woman (a literary agent and a person of considerable sophistication) who said "When I go to the movies, I just want to be entertained. I go to escape from my problems and the real world.'' This is a common attitude, I might add. Many people think that popular culture is just a way of ''killing time'' or amusing themselves and that it has little significance or impact on their lives or society at large.

There are, it goes without saying, some films that deal directly with political figures or social problems and, obviously, have political content to them. But my argument is that all films, television shows, and entertainments have a political dimension to them, whether we recognize it or not. For all our popular culture (and our elite culture as well, I might add) deals with values people have and connects, ultimately, to the social arrangements and attendant political cultures that shape our view of things.

In this context, media texts function in a number of ways: they reinforce certain political values and beliefs, they increase group solidarity and identity, and they help prevent dissonance and alienation. These mass-media texts, (and popular culture in general) then, play an important role in our political formation. I have been dealing with the mass media and popular culture, but one might broaden the discussion and consider the relationship that exists between communication, of all kinds, and politics. What relation exists, we may ask, between the two larger domains that now suggest themselves— political science and communication theory? I will begin with a brief discussion of communication theory.

Communication Theory

We have been most ingenious in developing theories about communication. Communication scholars tend to feel that communication is central to understanding everything else and have generated innumerable theories of communication and models of the communication process. In a brief book, *Introduction to Communication Studies*, John Fiske lists six important communications models: Shannon and Weaver's *Mathematical Theory of Communication*, which focuses on message transmission, George Gerbner's model, Lasswell's model (''*Who* says *what* in *which channel* to *whom* with *what effect*?'') Newcomb's model, Westley and MacLean's model, and Jakobson's model—and those are only a few of the models available.

From these various models I have selected some of the more important concepts that help us understand communication, in the broadest sense of the term.

Communication Involves a Transfer of Information

For Shannon and Weaver, communication involves an information source (with a message), a transmitter (a transmitted signal), a channel (which can be affected by "noise," something not intended by the sender), a receiver (a received signal), and a destination (message receiver). Information is understood as being tied to unpredictability. If a message is not unpredictable, according to this model, it is not seen as information.

This Information Is Transferred from a Sender to a Receiver

Here Jakobson's model is useful to examine. As Fiske writes, Jakobson starts with a linear base:

> An *addresser* sends a *message* to an *addressee*. He recognizes that this message must refer to something other than itself. This he calls the *context:* this gives the third point of the triangle whose other two points are the addresser and the addressee. So far, so familiar. He then adds two other factors: one is *contact*, by which he means the physical channel and psychological connections between the addresser and addressee. The final factor is a *code*, a shared meaning system by which the message is structured. (Fiske 1982, 36,37)

A diagram of this model follows:

FIGURE 10.1
Jakobson Model of Communication

Addresser————————————————————Addressee
Context
Message
Contact
Code

The Information Is Encoded and Decoded

This is dealt with in Jakobson's model. The information transferred is put into a form by the sender that is intelligible to the receiver. This is not always as simple as it might seem. The distinguished Italian semiotician Umberto Eco has suggested, for example, that with the mass media, there is a great deal of aberrant decoding by audiences who don't understand many of the references, allusions, and ideas of the encoders (who produce films, television programs, and other kinds of mass media). We would do well to keep this in mind, for it suggests that people play an active role in interpreting communications and are not simply passive receivers of media content who all understand or interpret it the same way, nor are they all affected the same way.

The Information Is Sent Via Some Medium

This can be thoughts (in intrapersonal communication, when we carry on internal dialogues with ourselves), speech or writing, or visual messages (in interpersonal communication), plus various aesthetic factors that are spread by electronic and other means (in mass-mediated communications). Marshall McLuhan argued that "the media is the message," and while this is somewhat of an exaggeration, McLuhan was correct in calling our attention to the aesthetic factors connected with mass-mediated communication. There are many things to keep in mind here in the case of such visual media as film and television: the kinds of shots used, the choice of shots, the cutting and editing, the use of lighting, color, sound, and graphics, the choice of language by the speakers, and the use of facial expression and body language by people.

The Information Has Some Effects

This matter was brought to our attention by Lasswell, who asked what the effects of communication were. As Fiske explains (1982, 32), what Lasswell meant by effects was "an observable and measurable change in the receiver." This concern with effects has dominated research on mass communications, Fiske adds. He writes:

Most mass communications research has implicitly followed this model. The work on institutions and their processes, on the producers of communication, on the audiences and how it is affected clearly derives from a process-based linear model.

The Information Has Some Functions

Here we enter into the sociological perspective. There are numerous uses and gratifications that people derive from communications (and the mass media, in particular); communication enables us to express our ideas and our emotions. And, in particular, by the processes of selective inattention and attention, we are able to reinforce our world views, confirm our identities, and avoid (to varying degrees) dissonance.

Functional explanations are consequence explanations. The consequences of a form of social organization and behavior in it, such explanations say, help maintain that way of life (or culture, if you prefer).

The Information Has Meaning

The discussion, to this point, has been on a rather linear process of transferring information between senders and receivers. What has been neglected, and this is of central importance I believe, is the matter of meaning. How do people make sense of communication? How do they find meaning in communication? What is meaning? It is here that semiotics, the studies of signs in society, comes into play. Semiotics (also known as semiology) concerns itself with how people find meaning in communication and focuses not on the channel of communication or the sender but on the *text* that is being communicated and the codes that are necessary to make sense of this text.

I will discuss some of the essential concepts of semiotics shortly, after my discussion of political science. I should point out, though, that this focus on meaning takes us away from a social psychological approach to media, which emphasizes individual personality, and a concern with quantifiable effects (such as opinion and attitude change) and suggests we consider other matters. By contrast, the Wildavsky-Douglas approach to political culture postulates an active perceiver who selects some phenomena in or rules others out in order to support his or her way of life. In short, messages do not impose themselves on people; instead, the process works the other way around. Who perceives what and why they perceive is the question.

On Political Science

What is political science and what should it concern itself with? This is not a simple matter, and in investigating the subject I discovered many commentators who pointed out that political science lacks a discrete identity. One way to understand political science is to compare it to some other social sciences, such as psychology, anthropology, and sociology. In Table 10.1 below I offer some of the basic concerns of each of these domains and suggest the process by which they work on people. Table 10.1 is highly schematic and is meant to show the most fundamental differences between the various social sciences.

In recent years there has been a good deal of merging among the various social sciences, so now we have political sociologists, social psychologists, political anthropologists, social anthropologists, and so on. One might add other social sciences and further complicate matters.

Seymour Martin Lipset has discussed the relationship that exists between political science and other social sciences in his book, *Politics and the Social Sciences*:

> Whether political science can or should attempt to formulate an analytically distinct theoretical system remains an open question. And although the concerns of the field increasingly overlap with the work of other fields this should not be taken as a threat to the autonomy of the discipline. Actually, the converse thesis could be argued. The political in the form of concern with the decision-making process, with the distribution of power, with the nature of legitimate authority, with the place of the state as the principal agency of collective action within society, with the analogy between the behavior of the voter and the buyer in the marketplace, has intruded into the work of other social sciences. (1969, xx)

This listing offered by Lipset gives us a pretty good overview of the main concerns of political scientists, though one might add a few other

TABLE 10.1
Basic Concepts of Various Social Sciences

Sociology	Political Science	Anthropology	Psychology
Institutions	Power	Culture	Psyche
Groups	The State	Values	The Mind
Socialization	Indoctrination	Enculturation	Internalization

concepts such as ideology, obligation, parties, interest groups, stratification, public opinion, and the issue of whether it is society or politics that is primary.

What is important to recognize here is that one way or another, the central concerns of political science (and, I might add, the other social sciences) are connected to, either directly or indirectly, communication and, increasingly so, the mass media. Karl W. Deutsch has even argued, in his influential book *The Nerves of Government: Models of Political Communication and Control* that "it might be profitable to look upon government somewhat less as a problem of power and somewhat more as a problem of steering; and . . . steering is decisively a matter of communication" (1966, xxvii)

I might point out that the study of communication also has a diffuse identity, like that of political science. Schools of communication are relatively recent arrivals in academia, and many of the most influential thinkers in these schools are people who have been trained in sociology, political science, history, literature, journalism, economics, psychology, and anthropology.

In recent years, people trained in semiotics (which we may identify with linguistics and philosophy), psychoanalytic theory, and Marxist and feminist thinkers (who have an ideological focus) have become more prominent. There is now a radical split in communications studies between those with a social science background whose interests have been described as *administrative* and those with ideological concerns, Marxist and otherwise, who have been described as forming a *critical* school. There is also room for all kinds of other approaches to communications study. These disciplinary orientations and ideological interests play an important role in determining the kind of research that is carried out.

But whatever the position of the researcher, administrative and critical communications scholars tend to agree on the importance of communication and particularly the mass media. Actually, the critical scholars have a vested interest in the notion that the media are strong and powerful since they tend to see the media as functioning ideologically—to generate "false consciousness" and maintain and preserve the status quo. Other scholars have gone back and forth on the matter of whether the media are powerful.

Elihu Katz, trained as a sociologist, has an interesting article "On Conceptualizing Media Effects: Another Look," which offers a brief history of how different notions of media effects have evolved. He suggests, in the case of television for instance, that the dominant paradigm (administrative) focuses too much on the viewer and neglects the text and that the critical researchers focus too much on the text and neglect the viewers; that is, critical theorists often assume they can read effects directly from their analysis of these texts.

In recent years, Katz tells us, there has been a convergence and, due in part to the influence of semiotic theory, researchers have come to recognize that both audiences and texts are important and that people make *dominant* and *oppositional* readings of texts. Neither "vulgar gratificationism" (Katz's term) nor "vulgar Marxism" seem to be terribly useful anymore.

Focal Points in the Analysis of Texts

Let me suggest that there are five areas or *focal points* we might consider in the analysis of any *text* (whether it be a conversation, a film, a novel, a television program, or whatever). These are: the text or work of art itself; the artist/creator of the text; the audience of the text; the society in which the text is created and distributed; and the medium of distribution. (These five focal points are discussed in detail in chapter 11.)

In this book, my main concern has been with analyzing texts and with the audiences (read members of *political cultures* here) of these texts. I have assumed that my audiences or political cultures make *preferred readings* of texts and are able to select texts that will be congruent with their political values. In some cases, such as "songs" that competitive individualists should like, it has been relatively easy to find excellent texts. *My Way*, which Frank Sinatra modestly describes as "the national anthem," fits very well. In the same way, "Russian roulette" fits ideally as a "sport" for fatalists. In other cases, however, it was difficult to find the perfect text.

I am positing *good* readers here—members of a given political culture who consume only the appropriate texts, ones that support or reinforce their political values and that help them avoid cognitive dissonance. There is the possibility, of course, that we will have *poor* readers, those who consume the wrong media texts but decode them aberrantly and, by misinterpreting them, do not realize that their values are being challenged. There is, or course, another possibility. We may have good readers who consume inappropriate texts and interpret these texts accurately; these readers are probably those who are marginal to their political cultures and are in the process of moving to another political culture.

I have focused my attention, then, on audiences and the texts they consume, and on the relationship that exists between texts (and by implication, communication and the mass media in general) and political beliefs. These beliefs, Wildavsky shows, can be derived from the primary consideration—people's social arrangements and the norms that support these social arrangements, that is, cultures.

Theories of Culture are Theories of Communication

Cultures, Wildavsky explains, are programmatic and have payoffs. He writes:

> Cultures claim that if the individuals involved act according to certain shared values, then they will do well in the world. Cultures contain programs enabling individuals to figure out how to behave and how to screen the environment so as to make their behavior efficacious. Rationality is culturally controlled in that individuals use their social relations to filter their environment so they can select appropriate objects of attention and value them accordingly. (1982, 11)

If the culture does not fulfill its contract and provide adequate payoffs, Wildavsky adds, parties can change affiliations.

He quotes Karl Popper's work *The Self and Its Brain* and discusses his notion that observations are "theory impregnated" and that theory comes before observation. For Wildavsky, it is the political culture that provides something analogous to a theory and that shapes the way people interpret reality.

Anthropologists have offered numerous definitions of culture; they have been as creative as communications scholars in working out definitions and theories of culture. They are almost unanimous in suggesting or implying that culture is intimately tied to communication. For culture to survive, it must be passed on from generation to generation, so communication is of necessity a central component of culture. And many anthropological studies concern themselves with such matters as beliefs, attitudes, values, the conceptual world of a people, as these phenomena are manifested in myths, rituals, songs, folklore, material objects, and other *imponderabilia* (the term is Malinowski's) of daily life.

What Wildavsky calls a *program* might also be called a *code* by which I mean a set of rules that enables one to interpret various phenomena; culture can be seen as a series of codes, each of which applies to some aspect of life. Wildavsky's four political cultures are, from this perspective, four sets of codings or culture codes that help people make sense of the world.

Wildavsky tells us that each political culture helps people answer such questions as "who am I?", that is, "what kind of group do I belong to?" and "what should I do (regarding prescriptions)?" Each culture must, he adds, differentiate itself from others, and it is here also that communication is implicated.

The semioticians tell us that we find meaning in the world by setting up relationships. "Concepts are purely differential," Saussure tells us, "and defined not by their positive content but negatively by their relations with other terms of the system" (1966, 117). We find meaning, in essence, by setting up binary oppositions. The basic characteristic of concepts, he adds, is "in being what others are not" (1966, 117).

Wildavsky's theory of culture is full of paired oppositions:

Grid (Rules)	**Group (Collectivities)**
Few prescriptions	Many prescriptions
Weak boundaries	Strong boundaries
Egalitarians	Hierarchical elitists
Competitive individualists	Fatalists
Social structure	Ideas, values, beliefs

The terms *grid* and *group* come from work by Mary Douglas, who developed a prototype of Wildavsky's four-celled figure and has used it, with a number of ingenious variations, in later work (including a book with Wildavsky, on risk). The matter of prescriptions and boundaries, Wildavsky suggests, are the two basic questions of social life, out of which the four political cultures are derived. I also distinguish analytically between the social arrangements in which people live and the ideas, values, and beliefs which, in his theory, justify these social arrangements. In real life, as we are wont to say, cultures are made up of people who share values legitimizing their desired social relations. As Wildavsky says, there are no disembodied values and no social relations without moral justifications.

I should point out that this theory allows for movement and change by the actors involved; it is not deterministic. Mary Douglas emphasizes this point in a discussion of her original grid-group formulation. As she writes in *In The Active Voice*:

> The interaction of individual subjects produces a public cosmology capable of being internalized in the consciousness of individuals, if they decide to accept and stay with it. This particular approach does not assume that they must. It is not an exercise to demonstrate the sociological determination of thought. If I were tempted in that direction I would have to face an insoluble problem in accounting for social change. As Durkheim saw, once he had explicitly developed the analysis of how social categories are internalized in the individual mind, he had no way of understanding private dissent. But this present argument allows plenty of scope for individual disagreement, rebellion, mustering of support to change the whole context, or of emigration from one place on the map to another more congenial. It presupposes that some mixture of self-selection and adaptation accounts for a fit between personality measurements and grid-group social position. (1982, 200)

She adds that she sees her analysis as not being anchored in any way but as floating "on the shifting interaction of intelligent subjects" (1982, 200).

Cultural theory, then, is not deterministic at all; it posits the possibility of movement and assumes a thinking "actor" who assesses payoffs and is generally capable of moving from one political culture to another (except for the fatalists, that is). In *The Nursing Father: Moses as a Political Leader*, Wildavsky shows how Moses makes a "U-turn" and travels through the various political cultures as he evolves.

People change political cultures because they have experiences that call into question the validity of the political culture and belief system that had been guiding them. As Wildavsky explains it:

> There are always experiences that run counter to the prevailing paradigm. Life (or science) cannot stand still while each and every one are [sic] tested. Otherwise there would be no stability. As anomalies accumulate, the individuals involved consider whether other theories or ways of life

might be superior. It is not that one fact is true and another false but rather that one theory with its associated facts eventually challenges and perhaps replaces another. (1982, 4–5)

Or, to put it another way, "a political act is rational if it supports one's political culture." We are, this theory suggests, guided by our reason and are capable of judging whether whatever theory we hold to is adequate to make sense of our experiences. This would imply, then, that the mass media, while powerful, are not as powerful as some media theorists would argue.

There are certain aspects of Wildavsky's cultural model of politics that suggest that it might also be looked upon, I would argue, as a cultural model of communication. As such it has a number of implications.

In an essay, "Reflections on the Lost Vision of Communication Theory," reprinted in Sandra Ball-Rokeach and Muriel G. Cantor's *Media, Audience and Social Structure*, Thelma McCormack writes:

> The cultural model assumes that we are symbol creators, that we think with our imaginations and fantasy, but what we are seeking above all, is meaning, a set of meanings that can be shared with others to form social bonds. . . . But meaning is not just created; it uses existing meanings embedded in tradition. The past, then, never vanishes; it is layered over so that what often seems like the new will continue to reach and touch a very wide group of people. In this way, the persistence and continuity of culture are ensured. When changes do occur, they are slow and selective, avoiding any normative conflict that could weaken the social cohesion. . . . To summarize, the cultural model is a conservative one: in part, because of its emphasis on normative integration; in part, because of its emphasis on cultural continuity; and, in part, because it sociologizes the political. (1986, 38)

For McCormack, the power of media stems not so much from the impact the media have on their audiences but on other media and other institutions. Power is, for McCormack, a central concern, yet ironically, she adds, "we have reached a period in our social history that is intensely political yet lacking a theory of politics and the media" (1986, 42).

It is to the subject of politics and communication (with a focus on the mass media) that I would like to turn, now. I will offer an introduction of some of the basic concepts of semiotics and a discussion of the process by which we find meaning in everyday life. Then I will consider the implications of this on communication in an analysis of what we might call the politics of the sign.

The Politics of the Sign

A sign can be understood as anything that can be used to stand for or represent anything else. The two most important approaches to signs come from the work of the Swiss linguist, Ferdinand de Saussure, and the American philosopher C.S. Peirce. Saussure divided signs into two components: sound-images (signifiers) and concepts (signifieds). The relationship that exists between signifiers and signifieds is arbitrary or conventional, which means we have to learn these relationships. Figure 10.2 shows this relationship.

Saussure saw symbols as a special case, and suggested that they are quasi-conventional. For example, the familiar symbol of justice (the blinded goddess with scales) is a much better symbol of justice, since it suggests fairness, than, say, a feather or an ink bottle.

In a classic formulation of the subject, Saussure wrote:

> Language is a system of signs that express ideas, and is therefore comparable to a system of writing, the alphabet of deaf-mutes, symbolic rites, polite formulas, military signals, etc. But it is the most important of these systems.

> *A science that studies the life of signs within society* is conceivable; it would be part of social psychology and consequently of general psychology: I shall call it *semiology* (from Greek *sēmeîon* "*sign*"). *Semiology would show what constitutes signs, what laws govern them. (1966, 16).*

FIGURE 10.2

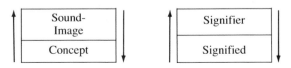

It is important that we notice that Saussure was interested in the way signs functioned *in society*; semiology is not an arcane science that has little relevance to society or politics.

I have already discussed another of Saussure's ideas—that concepts derive their meaning from relationships and not from some "essence" they have or exemplify.

The other basic formation comes from Peirce, who developed what became the science of semiotics. Peirce suggested that there are three kinds of signs: icons, which signify by resemblance; indexical signs, which signify by cause and effect relationships; and symbols, which are purely conventional. His work on signs is exceedingly complicated, but his trichotomy is of central importance to his work. Signs—words, symbols, images, visual phenomena of all sorts—are the basis of semiotics.

Table 10.2 below, taken from my book *Media Analysis Techniques*, shows how the three kinds of signs function.

There are a number of other concepts that are needed to gain a basic understanding of signs and the way they function. (The science of semiotics is, I should point out, an extremely complicated one and there are volumes upon volumes of theoretical works as well as applied works, journals, learned societies devoted to the subject, and so on.) These are:

Metaphor

Communication by analogy.

TABLE 10.2

	Icon	Index	Symbol
Signify By	Resemblance	Causal connection	Convention
Example	Photograph	Smoke/Fire	Words Flags
Process	Can see	Can figure out	Must learn

Metonymy

Communication by association.

Paradigmatic Structure

The hidden sets of paired oppositions found in texts, which reveal their latent meanings.

Syntagmatic Structure

This stems from the work of Vladimir Propp, who argued that all tales have a limited number of functions (acts by characters) which are the building blocks of narratives.

Codes

Collections of rules for interpreting signs. Highly complex patterns of associations which we learn in a given culture. The realm of the mass media is one in which there is a great deal of "aberrant decoding," which means that audiences are not monolithic, that individuals and subgroups or subcultures often interpret texts differently from the ways the creators of texts intended them to.

Intertextuality

The relations of texts to previously created texts. We often read one text in terms of other texts we know that are relevant to it. A good example would be parody, which involves a humorous imitation of some text.

The central concern of semiotics is how people find meaning in the world, how they make sense of signs. And, as Umberto Eco has pointed out, if signs can be used to tell the truth, they can also be used to lie. We must always be on guard when we interpret or read signs—or texts, which are systems of signs.

The realm of politics and the realm of semiotics each can be seen as ovals that intersect, giving us a realm that we might understand as the realm of the politics of the sign.

Semiotics and culture can be joined. What the cultural theory I have been explaining conveys is rules for assigning meanings to symbols. Anything can be symbolic. What counts, first, is conflict over meaning, and second, that this conflict is about rival ways of life contending for supremacy by making their meanings prevail. If there are just four viable cultures, there are four sets of symbols in competition.

"This universe is perfused with signs," Peirce has said, "if it not composed exclusively of signs" (quoted in T. Sebeok, 1977). Whatever else we may be, we are sign-making and sign-interpreting animals. We are Homo sapiens, which might broadly be defined as people who know or think, and what we know or think is, in the final analysis, a product of how we interpret signs. The questions that Wildavsky suggests are the fundamental ones we ask, "Who am I?" and "What should I do?" are, then, semiotic questions as are, semioticians would argue, ultimately all questions. (Semioticians may be good democrats but their science is an imperialistic one.)

The concepts I have just listed have one thing in common—they are all connected to society, are tied to our social experience. We read texts in terms of the codes we know, in terms of our familiarity with other texts, that stems from our fund of knowledge and experience (from our social situations), and in terms of our beliefs and values.

Most of the time, of course, we are not conscious of what we are doing when we interpret signs and function as semioticians; we are like Moliere's character who never realized he was speaking prose. We are untutored and un-self-conscious semioticians, but semioticians we are, whether we know it or not.

Mark Gottdiener, a sociologist, makes an interesting point about the relation between semiotics and social relations. In an essay "Hegemony and Mass Culture: A Semiotic Approach," published in the *American Journal of Sociology*, he writes:

> Following Saussure, the production of meaning takes place only by virtue of a social relation, because language is a sui generis social construction. Although other approaches focusing on interacting subjects use a situation-

FIGURE 10.3
The Realm of the Politics of the Sign

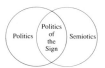

al conception of social interaction, the object of analysis in semiotics is the socially sustained system of signification, including its material objects and their interdependencies, that produces and sustains meaning through socio-structural interaction. (1985, 985)

Semiotics is not some kind of abstract science of signification; it is grounded in our social relations and experiences. He adds,

People are the bearers of all meaning, either in the isolation of personal use or as the product of complex social processes of group interaction. (1985, 986)

His essay, which attacks many of the presuppositions and limitations of the Marxist theory of hegemony, uses the concept of "transfunctionalization" to support his argument. He explains this concept as follows:

According to this perspective, a distinction is made between the use of objects to fill their immediate function and a socially sustained use of the object, which produces a second-order meaning for that object. It is the secondary use that creates signification, and this process is a social one. Furthermore, when the second-order use of objects is explicitly designed to signal a message, communication (intentionality) as well as signification is said to be present. (Gottdiener 1985, 988)

It is this which explains, I believe, why people are often so unaware of the signifying functions of objects (by which we can read mass-mediated texts and other phenomena). We look at their immediate function and neglect other aspects, namely their signifying functions.

Gottdiener mentions the work of the anthropologist Marshall Sahlins approvingly and writes:

Sahlins, in particular, has insisted productively that human behavior is always meaningful and that, consequently, social life is organized first and foremost around systemic, symbolic modes of interaction. . . . Thus, group life possesses its own "relative autonomy" from economic and political processes. The impact of mass culture must always be understood within the social context of this ongoing, localized process of meaning creation and group interpretation. (Gottdiener 1985, 991)

We are very close, I would argue, to Wildavsky's formulations about the four political cultures and the power of group affiliations to color people's interpretations of the world and political decision making.

Let me discuss an important aspect of mass media (and culture in general) here—images. They play, I believe, a central role in giving people a sense of political identity.

Images are hard to pin down. We can use language to describe something and generate an image. And we can look at the way businesspeople or politicians or professors are described in some body of literature to determine an *image* (by which we mean some kind of generalized picture of). But most of the time, when we use the term image, we refer to a visual image, a visual representation of something. The different media generate different kinds of images: television images are a series of dots that are always moving, cartoons are line drawings, photographs are made of small dots that don't move, film images are essentially photographic negatives, paintings are collections of dots and lines, areas of color, etc.

Much of our information about the world comes from visual images; when we see, we see images (though we see selectively and do not regard with equal interest or intensity every aspect of every image that is available to us). One of the most important kinds of images is the symbol—an object that has conventional meaning and that often carries a great deal of emotional "baggage" with it. This is because symbols are generally intimately connected to historical and social experiences and events and have the power to regenerate the emotions connected with the original event. Symbols activate memory and make use of knowledge we all have.

Through images our values are affirmed and made intelligible. And that is why, for example, political campaigns are so dominated by television, the most powerful generator of visual images and sound, and thus the most powerful medium we experience in our daily lives. We spend something like 80 percent of our mental energy processing visual images, or to use the semiotic term, *reading* them.

In terms of political behavior, I believe we read images to determine those who are like us, relative to our political cultures, that is, and those who aren't. Once we make that determination between "we" and "they," everything else becomes relatively easy. It is like the famous Seven-Up uncola campaign. What is Seven-Up? The campaign didn't tell you, but it did tell you one thing—it was an uncola.

Wildavsky tells us that people only need to make a couple of determinations to be able to make all kinds of political decisions. Am I a member of a strong group, bound and limited in my decisions, or am I free to negotiate for myself? That is the first. The second is whether society prescribes behavior for me or my socially fixed obligations are weak and few.

Much of this, I suggest, is done by symbolic means and by visual images found in the media. One of the complications here is that we may misread images and symbols and that political leaders may try to confuse us by tailoring their images to suit their perceived audiences, to the extent that this is possible.

I have tried to show, in my analyses of the various texts dealt with in this book, how we can find political content in areas where we don't expect to and how these texts function in the general scheme of things. In a sense, then, the term "representative" government is doubly meaningful. We elect people to serve as our representatives in various legislatures (and there are various theories about how representatives should function in democracies). But we also elect people on the bases of representations, or should I say pictorial representations or visual images that come to us through the mass media.

I hope that my study of our popular culture and mass media has revealed their political dimensions and suggested something about how they function. Aaron Wildavsky's work on political cultures has provided me with a way of tying the values found in specific works to particular groups of people, those who make up his four political cultures. I see this book as just a beginning step in a subject that demands much more scholarly attention—a comprehensive theory of politics, culture, and communication.

Dear Dr. Berger:

While wandering through the stacks at Central Library, looking for a book for my freshman composition class, my eyes fell upon your book, "Pop Culture." I took it out and read it the same night. It was wonderful. You brought out many things which are always on my mind, always disturbing me.

As a freshman in college, and thus justifiably undecided as to what I shall end up "doing," I find it increasingly difficult to consider any one topic more interesting than another. But there are several things I already know, just by being alive in today's world. Popular culture inundates us; it is us. What have we to strive for, except numerous credit cards, a two-car garage, and white teeth? Stripped of these things, most Americans would feel they were no longer human.

However hard I try to remain aware of popular culture, and criticize it continuously, I am nevertheless sucked in. There is no way not to to be drawn into the flow of it. It is the easiest way to live—complacently. Southern California, especially (I was raised in Massachusetts), is ideal for a leisurely, material oriented existence.

My reason for writing to you (actually, I'm not quite sure why I write to you, but you seemed the suitable person to turn to) is to ask if there is a line of study one can follow in order to understand these strange phenomena, such as chewing gum. It is all so disturbing; there must be somebody equally as disturbed as I, possibly a group of them, already studying it. But where are they? And is it possible for them to have any noticeable effect on the American public? Before we bury ourselves in McDonald's hamburgers and pet rocks, perhaps we shall see the light? But what does the light consist of, and how do we extricate ourselves from this mess?

—Portion of letter from student, March 12, 1976

11

Making Sense of Media: Focal Points in Analyzing Texts

The Focal Points Listed and Described

When we think about a work of art (henceforth to be known as a "text") we should always think about the medium that is "carrying" it. Each medium imposes specific limitations on a text. The television screen is small and image resolution is relatively weak; this means television tends to be a close-up medium with much of the action taking place along the Z-axis. But television also has a number of positive aspects: it is easy to vary the shots, to manipulate lighting, and the costs are much less than film.

There are, in addition to the text and the medium, other matters (or focal points) to consider: the artist or creative personality behind a given text, the audience for whom the text was created, and the society in which the text is created. We find ourselves, then, with five focal points to consider in any analysis of a text or a medium:

A. *Art* (the text)
B. *Artist* (the creative personality most responsible for the text)
C. *Audience* (the people for whom the text was created)
D. *America* (the society in which the text is created)
E. *The Medium* (which carries and shapes the text).

I have used alliteration in this list as a means of helping us remember the focal points. It is important to keep in mind that all of these focal points interact with one another. In any given discussion or analysis of a text and a medium (which is where we usually start) we can also consider the text and the artists, the text and the audience, the text and society.

In the same manner, we can focus on the artists and their relation to the intended audience, to society, and the limitations and empowerments generated by the medium they use. We might focus on the audience and its relation to society in general and the medium. And finally we might focus on society and the medium.

We find, then, that we have ten different sets of two-way relationships that we might consider. These are:

1. *Art/Artist*   (AB)
2. *Art/Audience*   (AC)
3. *Art/America*   (AD)
4. *Art/Medium*   (AE)
5. *Artist/Audience*   (BC)

6. *Artist/America*   (BD)
7. *Artist/Medium*   (BE)
8. *Audience/America*   (CD)
9. *Audience/Medium*   (CE)
10. *America/Medium*   (DE)

It is these two-way relationships that I will explore now, in the belief that these relationships furnish us with a useful way of making sense of media and the texts we find in them.

Art and the Artist (AB)

In considering texts and those who create them, we find that there are numerous variables that have to be considered. In certain media, such as television, the creative process is often based on teamwork, and there is some disagreement as to who is the most important creative force behind a given work (an episode of a program, for example). There is a tendency now to argue that it is the director who is most responsible for a program being the way it is and looking the way it does. The medium, then, plays a role even though our focus is on a given text and the artist(s) who create that text. Certainly that is the case in media where collaborative efforts are the norm, such as television and film.

In certain cases, such as the novel, the situation is less complicated: there is a writer, who is unquestionably the auteur (though writers, in some cases, are influenced and modify their works as the result of a relationship with an editor or some other person) and there is the text itself. While the typeface and the design of the book play a role, this role is relatively insignificant.

The most direct relationship between an artist and a text can be found, it would seem, in the fine arts, where painters and sculptors (and other kinds of artists) work in a certain medium (oil painting, marble) and completely control the situation.

There are several topics of interest when we deal with the art/artist relationship. For one thing, there is the element of biography and what we might describe as the social formation of the artist. Artists are born into families in some class, have certain kinds of personalities ("creative"), and have certain political beliefs and ideologies that often have a major impact on their lives and work. Think here, for example, of the way political ideology has informed the work of Eisenstein, Orozco, Ayn Rand, and various feminist writers.

In looking at a work of art, especially one that has strong ideological content, there is always the question of what the artist believes; this is especially the case when we look at works from certain Marxist countries, where artists are usually required to adopt certain ideological positions. But it might also be argued that the same applies in the Western world, where audience acceptance (as opposed to political power and patronage) might shape the ideological content of a work. Think of Ian Fleming's spy novels and the role of James Bond as a symbol of England, the West, and capitalism (as well as racism and sexism, I might add).

According to the "critical thinkers" and Marxist critics (the two are not always synonymous), the texts we find in the bourgeois western societies, especially in the electronic and mass media, are loaded with ideology, even if it is not always apparent.

As for creativity, that is something of an enigma. We don't know why certain individuals develop the capacity or have the desire to create works of art. We know that creativity is involved with matters like sublimation, being unconventional and being willing to "break set," and we have numerous books by psychiatrists and others on the creative process, but it still is something of a mystery to us.

We must also keep in mind that even though works of art are created by individuals who sometimes are only trying to satisfy themselves and vent their creative forces, artists are also affected by their social class, by the social belief structures, political ideologies, and political cultures that are dominant when they grow up and do their work and by other societal pressures. There is a tension between individual volition (as it were) and social forces, between culture and personality, in the works that artists mysteriously generate.

Art and the Audience (AC)

This is the area where we find a good deal of mass communications research. Scholars want to know what effects media have on audiences, but the concern is really with texts and programming. Thus, for example, a great deal of research has been done about the effects of exposure to violence on television. But violence does not exist by itself; it is always found in some text or texts carried by some medium.

These texts are lumped together in many content analyses into what might be called a meta-text, television programming. This meta-text is then analyzed in terms of the number of violent incidents per hour or in terms of some other quantifiable topic. However, researchers seldom consider the aesthetics involved in each incident of violence, which often affects the way the violence is interpreted by viewers.

Let me offer an analogy. Suppose one were doing a content analysis of print, looking for the use of a certain word. Wouldn't it make a big difference if the word were found in bright red or in 72-point type? I believe it would, just as the *way* a given incidence of violence is shown (I almost said shot) makes a difference. The camera work, the editing, the lighting, and the sound effects all have an impact. Yet, generally speaking, all this is neglected—perhaps because it is too difficult to quantify it.

At one time we assumed that all audiences interpreted a given text in a similar manner and the message got through directly. This theory, sometimes known as the "hypodermic theory," is now considered by most scholars to be inadequate. We now talk about *reader response* and the way audiences *decode* a text. What this means is that the transfer of ideas and information is not automatic or direct; instead it is (literally) mediated and interpreted in different ways by different people.

There is the problem that I have already discussed of *aberrant decoding*, which involves misinterpreting various aspects of texts. It takes place when the codes of the creators of texts are different from those of the receivers of the texts. According to Umberto Eco, the distinguished semiotician and media theorist, the mass media have made the problem of aberrant decoding an important one. In the past, when print was supreme, the social backgrounds and knowledge bases (and, in turn, the codes) of the writers and the readers generally were much closer. Now, in an age of mass media, this is no longer the case.

Those who create films and television programs and other texts must keep their potential audiences in mind. In the case of a typical novel, which probably will be purchased by a few thousand people, the audience will probably be able to read the text without too much trouble. In the case of a television show, on the other hand, which might be seen by thirty million people, aberrant decoding is a much bigger problem. What happens most of the time, I would suggest, is that audiences are able to get most of the decoding right; they might miss a few things, but that is not terribly important as far as their pleasure is concerned.

It is the power of texts carried by media to socialize people that concerns many media scholars. We are all affected by powerful or appealing figures with whom we identify, and if the actions and values of these figures and the roles they play destroy our well being, there is good reason to be critical of television (which really means television texts or programs). "Television" is a shorthand way of saying television programs, including commercials. We know that young people, whose values are being formed, watch something like twenty-five hours of television programming per week. These programs and commercials (which are the most important genre of programs on television) must play an important role in socializing our young people. How to determine what that role is and the impact of television programs relative to other socializing forces (parents, peers, priests, professors, etc.) is an important problem for media researchers.

In talking about the impact of mass-mediated texts (especially television shows, films, and songs) it is also useful to talk about *acculturation*, which is an anthropological term. These texts carry "culture," which refers to the values and beliefs found in a given culture (or subculture) which are passed on from generation to generation. They also are tied to political cultures, as I've suggested. It is naive to think of these texts as mere entertainments; they are much more powerful than that. Television, our preeminent mass medium (in terms of hours of exposure and power), is an agent of culture; it performs the same tasks that were done by myths and legends in earlier days (and are still done in preliterate cultures today).

I believe an anthropological approach, which looks at belief systems and values, is an important corrective to the social-psychological studies of the past. These studies looked at attitude formation and opinions and matters like that. They have their value, of course, but they tend to neglect aesthetic considerations and the long-term cultural impact of texts on individuals and groups (subcultures). They also neglect the impact of groups on the interpretation of texts, especially as far as political values are concerned.

I am suggesting, then, that mass-communications research must not forget about texts in its desire for quantification. Not all acts of violence are the same, and any research that is unable to differentiate between different ways violence is presented in texts is deficient.

Art/America (AD)

Now it is time to discuss the relationship that exists between a text and society in general. I have used America as the society under consideration for two reasons: first, there is the matter of mnemonics and keeping the alliteration I have developed and second, and more importantly, it is American society that I know most about and that is the subject of so much media research.

The Marxist school of media research (and its allies in the so-called Critical school) focuses its attention on the role media plays in society, with particular reference to concerns such as the ideological content of media and the role it allegedly plays in shaping the consciousness of those who partake of the media. I would argue that we must look at particular texts rather than media in general—texts that are representative of the dominant program types or genres in a given medium and texts that are very popular and, quite likely, have a considerable impact on society.

By sampling dominant genres through the most popular and significant texts we can gain a better understanding of the role these texts play in society. (In some cases, such as television news programs, the genre is more important than any one broadcast and we have to put our emphasis there, though I would argue that it is always useful to use specific shows to support contentions about a genre and a medium.)

From the Marxist perspective, the media are instruments by which the dominant classes, who own and control the media, transmit their values, beliefs, and ideologies to the rest of society. Marxist critics have, in recent years, abandoned the notion of manipulation as too simplistic. Marxists argue that the ideological messages found in the media are believed by both those who own and control the media and those who are seen and heard in the media. That is, there is not conscious manipulation going on but, instead, the unconscious transmission of ideological notions that are held by owners.

The central notion of this ideology is that capitalism is desirable and so are all the beliefs and notions connected to it, such as individualism and the free market economy. It is the mode of production and the economic relations that obtain in a given society (what Marx called the ''base'') that shape, in complicated ways, the institutions and beliefs found in that society (what Marx called the ''superstructure'').

Because of the consolidation of media ownership (in newspapers, magazines, book publishing, television and radio, cables, etc.), a relatively small group of people control the media. And this small group of people, who form the dominant or ''ruling'' class through its ownership of the mass media, shapes the beliefs and attitudes of the masses. As Marx put it:

> The ideas of the ruling class are, in every age, the ruling ideas; i.e. the class which is the dominant *material* force in society is at the same time its dominant *intellectual* force. The class which has the means of material production at its disposal, has control at the same time over the means of mental production. (1964, 78)

The power of the media to shape our awareness of things, to set the agenda, to reinforce certain notions and denigrate others, all serves the interest, so the Marxists argue, of the ruling class.

This notion assumes that the media are powerful and do, in fact, play an important role in shaping our consciousness. If the media are weak, as some scholars argue, then controlling them would not be terribly important or useful. The best way to put the Marxist argument to the test, I believe, is to examine some of the more important texts and genres, and see what one finds. One might ask the following questions: What are the dominant values and beliefs found? What are the political implications of these values and beliefs? What issues and topics are neglected and not dealt with? What groups are underrepresented or neglected? What overt political biases are to be found? How are all these phenomena transmitted in specific texts? What significance do various genres have here? Do genres have political implications?

In the case of newspapers, for example, it is often suggested that one only finds political bias in the editorial sections, which are read by a relatively small percentage of readers. But this neglects the matter of which articles the newspaper chooses to print and which it doesn't, how the headlines are written, and the way articles are written—all of which have an impact on readers. In many countries, newspapers have a specific political position and are often allied with political parties: there are communist newspapers and conservative newspapers, and so on. Readers know beforehand that the newspaper will be ideological (by which I mean "supporting a coherent socio-political program").

This is different from the situation in America, where newspapers generally claim to be objective and nonideological or nonpartisan. What can be said of newspapers also can be said of magazines and the press in general—and, in particular, of television news; it selects certain stories to cover and it covers them in certain ways, and this has an impact on the way people view politics and see the world.

In the case of television bias is particularly important, since many Americans seem to get most of their news from television. The Marxists argue that even though television journalists are professionals who are "calling the shots as they see them," and are not consciously ideological, the ultimate impact of the news is ideological since these journalists all have been indoctrinated with a bourgeois (another word for capitalist) perspective on things and are unaware that they are carriers and perpetuators of this "bourgeois ideology."

One need not be a Marxist or "critical" theorist to ask the questions listed above. For example, what is the relationship between the values found in the media and "national character," the basic assumptions, values, and beliefs found in a given country? Do the media reflect (and in so doing reaffirm and reinforce) our basic values, or do they subtly "affect" our basic values by highlighting and thus supporting certain values and beliefs and neglecting others?

It would seem logical to assume that people would want to have their basic beliefs and values supported and reaffirmed by the media they consume, but it is also possible that those who create the television programs and write and perform the music and own and determine the editorial policy of newspapers and magazines may be able to shape, modify, and affect our values and beliefs. In the case of television news, for example, it has been argued that what is on the news "sets the agenda," determining what the public considers important and the positions people take on issues.

In addition to the political aspects of television, there is now increased attention to ethical considerations: what responsibilities do those who own, control, and work in the media have to the general public? What should be done about deceptive advertising, about programming for children, about the stereotyping of women, minorities, and the aged found in the media? What impact is the media (and particularly television) having on the political process and what should be done about things? There is much debate about the "imperatives" of television and the way it shaped the 1988 presidential campaign. Is it ethical to turn an important political process into a series of "sound-bites" and "attack commercials" and neglect the issues?

One problem is that ethics is a motherhood issue. Everyone is for being "ethical" but beyond that there is a great deal of disagreement about what being ethical means. What is unethical to one person might be ethical to another.

Let us move on to the next consideration, the relationship that exists between a text and the medium that carries it.

Art (Texts)/Media (AE)

This is an important topic that is often ignored or undervalued. Many scholars assume that a medium plays no significant role and essentially transports a text to its audience. It is true that the media "carry" texts, but it is not true that the media have little impact on them.

What we are talking about here is the matter of aesthetics. In some cases, such as books, the aesthetic impact is less important than in other areas, such as television. It does not make a big difference, generally speaking, if a novel is printed in Bodoni or Garamond, though the typeface, the spacing between lines, and the design of the book do have an impact. On the other hand, in film and television, the way something is shot always makes a difference. We know that considerations such as lighting, editing, the kinds of shots used, and sound make a film what it is. In the electronic visual media, such as film (which is increasingly being shot in video) and television, visual considerations are at least as important as narrative ones, and perhaps even more important.

Although the camera never lies (though with the development of computer imaging, all kinds of manipulations are possible with photographs and with film and television shots), what the camera chooses to focus on and the angles and kinds of shots presented affect how people interpret what the camera shows them.

It was the lighting and the camera that were mostly responsible for Richard Nixon's "losing" his television debate with John F. Kennedy. If the lighting had been different (and his makeup better), he would not have looked as seedy as he did. And the camera might not have picked up so clearly his facial expressions, which put so many people off. As studies have shown, those who listened to the debate on radio thought Nixon won. It was the people who watched Nixon on television and saw him looking disreputable, as if he needed a shave, who thought Kennedy had won.

The media shape the texts they carry. As I mentioned earlier, a small television screen necessitates a different kind of shot selection than a large movie screen does. You can do all kinds of things on radio, the so-called theatre of the mind, that you can't do on television. That is because you have to show things on television whereas you can ask people to imagine almost anything on radio.

The same applies to what people can imagine when they read books. Ironically, it is the image, as found in film and television, that limits imagination. One can imagine just about anything, which is why many people argue that novels should never be illustrated. Better to let people imagine what the various characters are like than show them what some artist thinks they look like. Once we see what a character supposedly looks like in a drawing, we find that our imaginations are unable to freely imagine that character.

There is also the matter of genres to consider here, for works of art in the mass media generally have a formulaic aspect to them. It is hard to say what a *genre* is with precision, but it involves some kind of work that has identifiable features and a recognizable structure.

In the case of television (the medium) we have a number of important genres (many borrowed from radio) such as news programs, situation comedies, soap operas, talk shows, comedies, science fiction, spy stories, westerns, police dramas, action-adventure shows, sports programs, commercials (the most important genre), and documentaries. Each of these genres has a number of particular characteristics that audiences recognize and that help them understand what is going on in the plot and what to think of various characters.

We find, then, that in westerns, which are no longer broadcast but which once dominated our airwaves, the following: the action takes place in a certain locale, at the edge of civilization; there are certain character types who are dominant (the heroic cowboy, the villainous professional killer, the schoolmarm, the preacher, the weak sheriff, etc.); the characters wear certain kinds of clothes (heroes in white and killers in black); and the plots have certain features such as chases on horseback, fistfights, gunfighting, etc.

All of these formulaic characteristics of the western help audiences make sense of what they see and help writers crank out scripts. There is, I would point out, a great deal of latitude in formulaic works despite the general characteristics they all share. What makes things easier for the writers is that they know that their audiences generally know what to expect.

Artist/Audience (BC)

Creative artists generally keep their audiences in mind. In the days when painters and sculptors were subsidized by royalty and the wealthy, artists had to please their patrons. The audience is of particular concern to those who work in the mass media, who measure success, in part, by how large an audience they can get.

This means that creators must be able to *encode* artists' works in a manner that large numbers of people can *decode* accurately enough so as to want to stay tuned to a television show or keep on reading a novel. The larger the audience, obviously, the greater the possibility that people will misinterpret what characters say and do or not recognize allusions made or simply not understand what is going on.

Nevertheless, even if individuals do misinterpret they often obtain enough pleasure from what they understand, or the sense *they* make of things, to be satisfied and keep tuned or keep reading. One might argue that all decoding is aberrant and that no two individuals ever interpret a story or commercial or anything the same way.

This is not only because there may be class differences between the members of the audience and those who create the works, but also because all individuals have lived different lives and have different stores of knowledge and different beliefs, so they see things differently. This does not mean they cannot interpret certain aspects of texts in similar ways, for quite obviously they can. But texts are so complex and complicated and so open-ended, generally speaking, that there is enormous room for what might be described as personalistic or idiosyncratic decoding, or decoding that is shaped by one's political culture.

There is also the matter of commercialism and the marketability of works to be considered. Obviously, if very few people can understand a text, it will not have a large market. But even texts that are quite simple often run into marketing problems, and in contemporary American society it is marketability that generally is the critical factor.

The mass media, the public arts, popular culture—all of these terms suggest some kind of a broad audience (broadcasting as opposed to narrowcasting). Traditionally it has been held, at least by many people, that the larger the audience, the lower the level of sophistication possible. To reach the largest audience you must provide it with texts that are at the level of the lowest common denominator.

Some scholars make a distinction between the two extremes of the continuum—the *fine arts* and the *mass-mediated* art forms. The fine arts, it is held, are those in which creators work essentially to satisfy themselves and their aesthetic impulses, while in the mass media, creators work essentially to satisfy the masses and gain little sense of accomplishment other than financial reward. In the fine arts we have experimentation, complexity, innovation, and true creativity.

In the mass-mediated arts we have, it is argued, simple-minded, formulaic hack work turned out as quickly as possible to feed the insatiable need of the media for "new" material. The fine arts, it is held, enrich and ennoble the human spirit while the popular arts cater to momentary whims; and being full of violence, racism, and sexism, the popular arts have mostly negative effects on people and destroy their well being.

The lists below shows these differences graphically:

The Fine Arts	The Mass Media
Complex	Simple-minded
Innovative	Conservative
True creativity	Formulaic hack work
Satisfaction of artist	Financial rewards of artist
Enrich people	Debase people

I think this set of oppositions may have some truthfulness to it, but it is a bit extreme. Consider, for example, the "serious" novel. There are many so-called serious novels that are second-rate pieces of work; and the same goes for poetry and other "fine" or "elite" art forms. It isn't the art form that is crucial but what one does with it. Thus, a so-called lesser genre, such as the science fiction novel or the detective novel, can be brilliantly written (and transferred onto film, as well).

Of course, you can't do as much with a comic strip as you can with a novel, but that is not a fair comparison. (In some cases, I might add, the comic strip might be a more satisfying text than a novel.) The important thing to do is look at texts individually and see what you find. I might also point out that people who study the mass media don't do so because of the aesthetic qualities of the texts but, instead, because the sociological and political aspects of these texts and the media that carry them are important. It doesn't make sense to argue taste when comparing a McDonald's hamburger and a gourmet French dinner. But if 7 percent of the American dining public eats at McDonald's every day, which happens to be the case, then we have a phenomenon of considerable importance.

The book-publishing industry is one in which recent changes in American corporations have had an important impact. We now have a great deal of consolidation in the book industry as giant publishing houses swallow up smaller ones so that now just a few gigantic publishers dominate American publishing. The impact of this phenomenon is hard to assess. In many (perhaps most) publishing houses it is the marketing director who makes the final decisions about what will be published.

That seems crass, but publishing is a business and publishers must make a profit to keep publishing. A book, in the final analysis, is a manufactured item that must be distributed and sold. Of course books are more than that. They are creative works written by people who invest a lot of themselves in their books, and sometimes these books have profound effects upon society.

There are also a number of small- and medium-sized publishers who undertake more adventurous books. The book publishing industry is hard to categorize because it covers both the fine arts and the mass media or popular arts, and often it is the profits made from the popular arts (example: the novels of Danielle Steele) that enable publishers to put out risky elite works such as first novels by ''serious'' writers, or books of poetry, which almost always lose money.

The moral of this disquisition is that while the audience does exert a certain amount of control over the artist, there is still a lot of latitude for creative individuals. We should also be careful about making generalizations about what the popular arts ''must be like'' and how they differ from the elite arts. Most of the work that is produced in any genre, art form, medium, or art level is second or third rate; it is possible to create works of interest and significance in almost all art forms.

Artist/America (BD)

Every artist is an individual, with a unique personality, but is also a member of society who has been influenced, on way or another, by that society. Artists (and by that term I mean all who use their creative abilities, regardless of the medium involved) are profoundly affected by the societies in which they grow up and by such sociological variables as social class, ethnicity, race, religion and sex (and sexual orientation). It is often useful, then, to know something about the biography of artists, about the details of their lives, for this often has an impact on their work.

But a person's perspective on things, world view, ethos, and life-style are also affected, in profound ways, by social movements and the kinds of institutions found in a society, and especially, it might be argued, their political cultures. Consider, for example, the matter of women writers. Before the development of feminism as a powerful and widespread movement, women writers with what we might describe as a feminist (that is, egalitarian) consciousness existed; but they tended to be isolated figures who could rely only on themselves. Now, with the development of a feminist consciousness and with feminism having become accepted and ''official,'' it is much easier to write feminist works, and many writers who might never have done so in the past are able to work in that tradition.

In addition, institutions now have taken over the role of the patron, in many cases. Most painters, sculptors, novelists, and poets survive by finding positions in universities; very few are able to survive on their own. In the case of the mass media, writers of films and television programs make a great deal of money, but it is extremely hard to find a position in these industries. The number of people in Los Angeles writing screenplays must be astronomical; the number of those who sell a screenplay is very limited.

Creative individuals are also affected by the level of aesthetic development found in their societies and by the age in which they live. For example, in the Middle Ages painters hadn't yet "discovered" perspective, and the paintings of the period, many of which are extremely beautiful, all are two-dimensional. It is only later in the Renaissance when painters had learned about perspective that artists were able to paint in this tradition. So creative people work within the bounds of traditions, though the great geniuses are able to transcend bounds and shape new ways of seeing things.

These traditions hold for a while and seem to dominate the way painters work until, somehow, new schools championed by innovators (who are often reviled at first) suddenly replace them. Think of the numerous schools of art in recent years, such as impressionism, cubism, abstract expressionism, pop art, and super-realism.

It is difficult to explain how it is that some creative individuals are able to break loose from the traditions that govern so many others. As I have suggested earlier, we have done a great deal of research on creativity but we still cannot fully explain it. The sociology of knowledge tells us that people's ideas of the world are based on those in the societies in which they grow up. If this were completely the case, we would not even know this. What happens is that some people are imperfectly socialized and others are "intellectuals" who are able to find ways of transcending the ideas of their period. The same applies to the arts.

In some societies, such as many of the Eastern European countries and Russia, where ideological considerations dominate all others, artists in every medium are generally little more than propagandists. The measure of a work of art is not aesthetic but the degree to which it is ideologically correct. There are some cases in which a creative person's ideological beliefs do not prevent great work from being created (as in the work of Picasso or Orozco or Eisenstein); in most cases, however, we find hack work when ideology pays the piper and calls the tune.

We find the same hack work in countries where the basic consideration is not ideological but commercial, as in Hollywood. Within the boundaries of the ideological and the commercial, however, there is still often room for artists to maneuver. There is something about the creative personality that resists domination and coercion. The great creative artists push this further and might be described as being revolutionary (in aesthetics if not in politics).

If artists reflect, in complicated ways, the societies in which they are born and grow up, they also often exercise a profound impact on societies. Jay Martin, an English professor at The University of Southern California and psychoanalyst has discussed what he describes as the *fictive personality*, one based on extremely strong identifications some people have with characters from novels, television programs, films, and the mass media in general. Unlike normal people, who adopt, momentarily, a number of fictive heroes and heroines, those with fictive personalities seem to fixate on one or two who shape their lives. We might wonder whether Martin is too optimistic in his assessment of so-called normal people; is it not possible that many people have adopted various characters as models for behavior and internalized their beliefs and values (or lack of values)? In the same way, visual artists, in giving us new ways of seeing things, also have a profound impact on us, even though the impact may take a while to show itself.

Artist/Medium (BE)

Creative artists of all kinds must consider their audiences. How much importance they give to them varies; those working in the mass media (which demand large audiences) are more affected by audience size and makeup than those in the elite arts, but the artistic process demands some attention to one's audience. The medium in which one works is also important.

One might think that the relationship that exists between artists and the medium in which they work is only aesthetic; that is not the case. For new mediums enable artists to do new things, and often what they do has a social and political significance. Thus, as John Berger has pointed out in *Ways of Seeing*, the development of oil painting allowed artists new scope in documenting the wealth and power of their patrons. He writes,

> The art of any period tends to serve the ideological interests of the ruling class. If we were simply saying that European art between 1500 and 1900 served the interests of the successive ruling classes, all of whom depended

in different ways on the new power of capital, we should not be saying anything very new. What is being proposed is a little more precise; that a way of seeing the world, which was ultimately determined by new attitudes to property and exchange, found its visual expression in the oil painting, and could not have found it in any other visual art form. (1972, 86–87)

This is because, he adds, oil painting has "a special ability to render the tangibility, the texture, the lustre, the solidity of what it depicts" (1972, 88).

This new medium, oil painting, could do things that other media could not do, and thus was able to serve a different function in society. So a medium, by expanding an artist's creative powers, also expands its social impact. That, at least, is John Berger's position. (His views are, it seems, influenced by Marx, who, as I pointed out earlier, argued that the ideas of the ruling class become the ideas of the masses. Those who control the means of mental production, including the arts, literature, and the mass media, shape those who consume these mental productions.)

The oil painting and other media of visual art that depend solely on the artist for execution have been joined by the photograph, which is now the dominant medium in our present era of mechanical reproduction. Photography is an expressive medium, not one that simply records. Photographers can use the power of the camera to take all kinds of shots, and they can do all kinds of things with negatives. They can select only certain portions of the negative to print, and they can manipulate the way the image looks by the way they process it. And now with computers they can manipulate and modify images to such an extent that we aren't sure that photographs are reliable as evidence.

You can see the impact of new technology in media such as film and television, where new cameras and simulation and special-effects techniques (many from computers) have greatly expanded the ability of film-makers and directors to create images that were never possible before. A film such as *TRON* (a technological triumph though not necessarily an artistic one) had something like fifty minutes of computer-generated special effects in it. TRON is a good case in point because it shows that while we have increased powers, new technology does not necessarily mean that what we create will have aesthetic merit.

A similar thing can be said about music. We have all kinds of new technology that composers can use, but this doesn't seem to help our composers do as good a job as Mozart or Beethoven or Bach did with pen and ink.

Marshall McLuhan, the Canadian media theorist, as I mentioned earlier, argued that the medium is more important than what is carried on it. His famous slogan was "The medium is the message." He believed that new media have profound effects upon our sense-ratios and the way we perceive the world, and it is this rather than the content that is all-important. I don't think he was right, but he did call attention to the power of the medium. The medium may not *be* the message, but it has a profound impact on it—and on the creative people who work in the medium.

There is a whole school of video artists who use the same technology as the people who work in commercial television, but the work of the video artists is considerably different. It is often avant-garde, it often parodies commercial television and film, it is experimental and often ideological. Their work shows that it is the not the medium that is dominant but the aesthetic sensibilities of the artists who employ that medium. The work of video artists often filters down to the commercial world and is appropriated by commercial television.

Audience/America (CD)

The audience for whom any text is created is a segment of the society in which the text is created. In the mass media, generally speaking, artists hope to please as large an audience as possible; but since commercial aspects are also important, artists also consider the demographics of that audience.

This is especially the case in radio and television where the function of the programming is to deliver an audience to the people who purchase the commercials, but it also applies to print media such as newspapers and magazines. It is the advertising that pays for the text, which leads me to suggest that the most important genre in most media is the commercial (in electronic media) and the advertisement (in print media).

Television commercials cost (relative to ordinary television production costs) an enormous amount of money, sometimes running as much as ten or more times the normal cost-per-minute of television programming. For example, the celebrated "1984" Macintosh commercial supposedly cost $600,000 to produce, for a minute's commercial. And to that you must add the cost of purchasing time to air the commercials in a campaign. Logic tells us that generally speaking there should be a match between the age, sex, class, and income levels of the audience for a given program and the products that are advertised. Demographics is destiny.

Recall, now, Aaron Wildavsky's suggestion that in democratic societies one finds four political cultures—groups who believe in certain ideas and values about society and the political order: these are what he calls *hierarchical elitists*, *competitive individualists*, *egalitarians*, and *fatalists*. We know from social science research that people tend to consume media that reinforce their beliefs and are congruent with their values. They select certain texts and avoid others. If they didn't do this, they would experience dissonance and be made uncomfortable by finding their beliefs, values, and world view under attack. All of this suggests that there are four relatively discrete audiences of media publics in any complex society, and that these audiences would only watch certain television programs, listen to certain radio programs, like certain records, read certain newspapers and magazines, and so on.

What pleasure, we might ask, would fatalists, who believe that life is based on chance and luck, find in watching programs in which the heroes and heroines embody middle-class effort optimism and believe (and even show) that people can create their own futures and shape their own destinies? Would egalitarians enjoy reading survivalist (fatalist) publications?

What happens, it would seem, is that many people who belong to each political culture either do not recognize the values in the texts they consume or they define their television viewing (and text consumption) as entertainment and therefore of little consequence. The average American who hasn't an articulated coherent political ideology, would probably find it amazing that he or she is considered a member of any of these four groups. These four groups are not tied to party membership; many affluent hierarchical elitists are members of the Democratic party and are statists who believe in the use of governmental institutions to solve social and political problems.

It is also possible that a given text can be decoded in a number of different ways, so that members of each of the four political cultures in American culture would see something different in a text such as a film or a football game. Texts are complex and polysemous, and it may be that we can all find something in most of them that would support our beliefs in one or another of the four political cultures.

There is an interesting typology that SRI International (once known as Stanford Research) developed called the VALS system—which focuses on people's Values and Life Styles—in order to determine what kind of appeals should be made to American audiences. The American public can be broken into three main categories and nine subcategories, each of which has different values, psychological traits, and lifestyle characteristics. This, it is argued, offers a refinement on the typical demographic categories.

We find then "need driven" people, who are "money restricted" (and are divided into "survivors" and "sustainers"), "outer-directed consumers" (who are "belongers," "emulators," and "achievers"), "inner directed" consumers ("I-Am-Me's," "experientials," and "societally conscious" groups) and at the top of the heap, a group with no subdivisions, "integrated" consumers.

What the people who developed VALS argue is that a commercial must be congruent with the values and beliefs of those it is directed to. Thus, Merrill Lynch, discovering that its target audience was "achievers" not "belongers" switched its campaign from "Bullish on America" (directed to "belongers") to "A Breed Apart" (directed to "achievers," who are affluent, independent, and have more money to invest than the essentially middle-class and more other-directed "belongers").

The basic problem with VALS, as I see it, is that it assumes that people always, or even generally, decode advertisements and commercials "correctly"—the way the advertising agencies and the companies they work for think they will. And even if they do, there is some question about whether "achievers" are, in fact, the best target audience for brokers. Maybe "belongers" are more easily persuaded to invest their money than "achievers." The VALS typology might therefore be leading to misdirected campaigns.

Audience/Media (CE)

In this section I will discuss the relation between media and various audience segments. Just as the American public can be broken down into value and lifestyle categories, it also can be broken into other kinds of groupings. Thus one can talk about "kidvid," the television directed to children, such as Saturday morning television, shows aired after school for children like *Sesame Street* and *Mr. Rogers' Neighborhood*, and various specials directed to audiences comprised mostly of children.

This matter of ''kidvid'' television is probably one of the most controversial and to my mind most disgraceful aspects of the television industry. Children are exposed to countless commercials that exploit their innocence and inability to evaluate what they see. Some programs in which characters are based on toys are little more than thirty-minute-long commercials. Children are seen as one more market segment to be exploited by advertisers as much as possible. They count on the legendary ''nagging'' power that children have to get them to force their parents to purchase the products that children have seen advertised such as cereals, toys, and food.

Young children watch enormous amounts of television, and while they do they eat. The situation is so bad that a national federation of pediatricians has made a short public service announcement trying to get children to *choose* the programs they want (instead of watching anything shown on television) and to be careful about eating too much. But how much chance does a thirty-second public service announcement have when it competes against hours of exciting animated films? Our young children become relatively passive viewers of television (even though there may be some activity while they watch). It is a far cry from the kind of play and activity that they really should have.

Certain genres tend to appeal to certain audience segments or demographic groupings; men watch more sports than women do, and women watch more soap operas and talk shows than men do (those women who are not working, that is). The young and the old watch a lot of television, since both groups tend to be isolated and have lots of time on their hands.

We see the incredible segmentation of the market in radio, where there are a number of different formats (all news, country and western, sports, beautiful music, talk shows, album-oriented rock, top forty, classical, golden oldies, and so on). As people mature they often migrate from one format to another, so that a teenager who listens to heavy metal rock may end up listening to beautiful music when middle-aged and talk shows when older.

Another phenomenon of some consequence here is connected to the development of new technology, which has a particularly strong impact on the television industry. We find the development of cable television and the spread of videocassette recorders and players has led to a weakening of television networks. There is some question about what will happen to television networks in the future and what role they will play.

People use their videocassette recorders to time shift and to watch what they want when it is most convenient. They also use their electronic tuners to zap commercials and skip from program to program so they are, in effect, watching television and not particular television programs. This is a revolutionary development, since the television industry is financed by the sale of commercials. It is no longer easy to "deliver" an audience to an advertiser since this audience now often switches channels as soon as a commercial appears.

Traditionally it has been the networks that financed television programs; but as cable television stations and networks prosper, they are increasingly involved in the production of programs. The auguries for the three television networks are not good. The question that many media critics speculate about, relative to television, our "cultural wasteland," is whether the changes that will take place in the structure of the television industry and the new roles that the networks will play will lead to improvements. We should be optimistic since it can't get any worse. Or can it? Since many of the networks own cable companies, we may end up getting more of the same, except that the distribution channels will be different.

America/Medium (DE)

We have now reached the last of the categories that emerges from putting the five major topics into various relationships—what is the relationship between a medium and America (or society in general)?

One of the most troubling developments involves the consolidation of media ownership and the lessening of competition. Ben Bagdikian of the University of California at Berkeley has spelled out the changes that have taken place in the media. In an essay, "The U.S. Media: Supermarket or Assembly Line," published in the Summer, 1985 issue of *The Journal of Communication*, he points out that by 1984 fewer than forty-four corporations controlled "half or more of all media output'' (1985, 100). The magazine industry is dominated by fewer than twenty corporations, and eleven (of the 2,500) book publishers control most of the annual sale of two billion books.

He mentions, in a statement to the Federal Trade Commission in 1984 that:

> Twenty corporations control 50 percent of all book sales. Twenty corporations control 76 percent of all record and tape sales . . . thirteen corporations control two-thirds of the audience in television and radio. Seven corporations control 75 percent of movie distribution.

And since he testified things have gotten worse rather than better and the media are experiencing greater consolidation. The one hundred men and women who control and run these media empires constitute, he suggests, "a private Ministry of Information and Culture for the United States."

This situation, he believes, imperils our democratic institutions, which depend upon the American people freely obtaining competing opinions about issues. The impact of this consolidation of control of the media is not always apparent, but think of the difference between those cities that now have but one newspaper and the situation that used to exist, when there were many competing papers that represented different political perspectives.

This concentration might seem trivial, but we live in a mediated society. We devote enormous amounts of time to the media. We watch, on the average, more than three and a half hours of television per day. We listen to the radio a couple of hours a day. We read newspapers and magazines, listen to records, and see films. This media is, to a great extent, a great enculturator; for many people popular culture is their culture.

Conclusions

This means we must recategorize media and popular culture. They are not just entertainments and therefore trivial. Instead, the media have an enormous impact on our bodies, our values, our politics, our lifestyles, and our societies. It is hard to get a good "purchase" on the mass media; there are so many different considerations, complications, and variables.

I hope that this exploration of the five focal points—the art, the artist, the audience, America (or society), and the medium—and the various relationships (ten in number) that obtain among them will provide those interested in the media with some useful and suggestive ideas. I hope, also, this essay will be a contribution that will help those interested in the media see directions for future research.

But if there is such a thing as a sense of reality—and no one will doubt that it has its raison d'être—*then there must also be something that one can call a sense of possibility.*

Anyone possessing it does not say, for instance: Here this or that has happened, will happen, must happen. He uses his imagination and says: Here such and such might, should or ought to happen. And if he is told that something is *the way it is, then he thinks: Well, it could probably just as easily be some other way. So the sense of possibility might be defined outright as the capacity to think how everything could "just as easily" be, and to attach no more importance to what is than to what is not. It will be seen that the consequences of such a creative disposition may be remarkable, and unfortunately they not infrequently make the things that other people admire appear wrong and the things that other people prohibit permissible, or even make both appear a matter of indifference. Such possibilitarians live, it is said, within a finer web, a web of haze, imaginings, fantasy and the subjunctive mood. If children show this tendency it is vigorously driven out of them, and in their presence such people are referred to as crackbrains, dreamers, weaklings, know-alls, and carpers and cavillers.*

—*Robert Musil,* The Man Without Qualities

12

The Pontifex of Pop: A Summary and Evaluation of My Research Program

"You don't grasp it at all. Not that I do myself. I would much rather not write the play at all."

"Then why not drop it?"

"How can I, dear? Don't be too obtuse. I must know who I am, mustn't I?"

"Surely your own play isn't going to tell you?"

"Of course not, dear; it's the critics who'll tell me. At the moment I don't exist; I don't even know what to become. *But once my play's done, I'll know. One critic will say 'Harold Snatogen reveals himself as an embodiment of the fashionable anti-Moon Goddess revival.' Another will say: 'In Snatogen see what Hegel called . . . ' and then he'll tell what Hegel called. After that it will be quite simple: I shall become the most flattering definition . . . and it has to be* printed. Speech is *useless.*

—*Nigel Dennis, Cards of Identity*

An Autobiographical-Theoretical Excursion

It is not often that I publicly evaluate my own work. Like Harold Snatogen and countless others, I've relied on critics (who know best, we must assume) to tell me who I am and what I'm really doing. This does not always comfort me. When my book *The TV-guided American* was published in 1974, it was reviewed by Jeff Greenfield in *The New York Times Book Review*. He concluded his review with a sentence I truly cherish, which went something like this—"Berger is to the serious study of television what Idi Amin is to tourism in Uganda.'' A good insult is infinitely more desirable than the faint-hearted and reluctant praise that tends to be the most I usually get.

I do not wish to suggest that I do not spend a good deal of time thinking about my work and myself. I have kept a journal for thirty-five years and now have more than fifty volumes in which I speculate about what I've written, what I'm writing, and what I will be writing. I write about other things as well—the weather, excellent meals I've had, etc., but mostly they deal with my writing and my efforts to ''peddle'' my manuscripts. So far I've written and edited something like fifteen books—which isn't bad for an amateur.

Thoreau, so the story goes, once had to buy five hundred copies of one of his books that his publisher couldn't sell. So he put them in his library. One day, when he was showing someone through his house, he said ''I have a library of 3,000 books, 500 of which I wrote myself.'' In the same light, I can say ''I am the author of sixty-five books, fifty of which are about myself.'' Thus, I am no stranger to writing about myself and my ideas, with something like 10,000 pages to my credit, but I haven't written these journals for publication. So this effort is something of a departure for me.

I chose this section on communication theory as an opportunity to try to make sense of my work (or my *ouevre*). I must confess at this time that I sometimes feel that I am really a humorist in sheeps' clothing as much of my work has elements of satire, parody, self-parody and whimsy. I am too kind-hearted to reject the null hypothesis —and some would say any hypothesis, and I lack ''the higher serious-ness.'' As a friend of mine, the late Stanley Milgram put it, I am ''an unclassifiable image.''

A Few Words on My Career

I received my B.A. in literature at the University of Massachusetts in Amherst, where I minored in philosophy and art. At that time the ''new criticism'' was popular, and I can recall using a textbook by Cleanth Brooks and Robert Penn Warren applying the new criticism to literature. I also studied with a fascinating man, Maxwell Henry Goldberg, who had come to the university to study chicken farming but ended up getting a doctorate in literature at Yale, if I remember correctly. His method was Rabbinic or Talmudic: he sometimes spent days and weeks on a paragraph, going over every word.

I spent years, it seems, pouring over the works of Matthew Arnold and Cardinal Newman dealing with culture and anarchy and related concerns. At that time I was very "literary" and wanted to "burn, with a hard, gem-like flame" as I sampled "the best that has been thought and said," or however Arnold put it. I was advised not to go into graduate work in English, as, so Goldberg and others said, I might find it too confining. So I decided to study journalism and applied to the University of California in Berkeley and the University of Iowa. That summer I drove to Alaska with a friend. I had heard that there was money to be made there. But things were tough, so I ended up flying down to Berkeley and going to summer school.

I had been accepted to Berkeley and intended to go there, but I was given a fellowship (part-time it turned out) at Iowa and ended up going there, where (since I was a proper Bostonian) I became the music and art critic for the *Daily Iowan* or, as I put it, "the cultural commissar of Iowa City." I also studied philosophy with Gustav Bergmann and participated in the Writer's Workshop, where I fell under the influence of Marguerite Young. I also continued with my art work and took a number of courses in painting.

After graduating from Iowa I was drafted, served two years in Washington, D.C. in a public information office there, where I also wrote high school sports for *The Washington Post*. After a year wandering around Europe (with money I saved), I decided on an academic career and went to the University of Minnesota, where I took a degree in American Studies.

I did most of my work in intellectual history (with David Noble), political theory (with Mulford Q. Sibley), and social and political thought (with Ralph Ross). I also continued to take philosophy courses and ended up grading papers for many of the professors in that department. I spent the year before I wrote my dissertation on a Fullbright in Milan, where I wrote a long content analysis of Italian weekly magazines, which was published in an Italian scholarly journal, *Il Mulino*, became friends with Umberto Eco (who was interested in the comics and popular culture in general), and got a good taste of Italian intellectual life. I returned to Minnesota and wrote my dissertation on Li'l Abner. It became my first book. I had written on this subject because I am an artist (and have drawn illustrations for *The Journal of Communication* for years) and because I am interested in humor. It was, for me, a natural subject.

I also wrote theatre reviews for *The Minnesota Daily* and occasional restaurant reviews and odd pieces. It was there, in 1963, that I wrote an essay, "The Evangelical Hamburger," in which I explained that McDonald's was "really" (in terms of its dynamics, that is) an evangelical religion and that it would soon take over the world. Everyone laughed!

My Interests

From my experiences in Milan and Minnesota I emerged with an interest in popular culture (and, in particular, popular texts), the mass media, everyday life, and the means for interpreting or making sense of these matters. I must confess that though I've been writing about popular culture for thirty years, I'm still not sure how to define it and how to differentiate (if one can, that is) between folk culture and so-called elite culture.

At the extremes, things are easy. Watching professional wrestling on television or going to a rock concert or reading a romance novel is popular culture and attending a poetry reading or a string quartet seems likely to be "elite" culture.

But what if the poetry reading and string quartet are broadcast on radio or television? I'm not sure it is profitable to spend much time debating about what is, what is not, or what may not be popular culture. It is much better and more useful, I've always felt, to look at specific works and genres (and related considerations) and analyze them.

This is not to say that I've never written about popular culture, per se, because I have. I once wrote an essay titled "Why Is Popular Culture So Unpopular?" and I've not hesitated, at times, from making what might be described as "sweeping generalizations" about popular culture and the media, as well as a number of other things. But generally speaking, I've always been more interested in looking at various examples of popular culture, doing what might be called "textual" criticism, than writing about what popular culture is or isn't and why we should study it. I don't feel I have to defend my interest in this field, though it may lack prestige. A glance at the offerings in many English departments, which now offer courses on science fiction, detective novels, popular fiction, etc., suggests that the battle is now over. The need for warm bodies and full classes cannot be resisted in most institutions and departments.

Most of what we call popular culture is, quite simply, trash. Not too many people will argue about that. So it doesn't make sense to castigate popular culture for being junk, sub-literature, etc. *The important question is this—what does this trash reveal about American (or any other) culture and society? And how do we find out what is revealed?*

W.H. Auden has written, in one of his poems, "prohibit the rehearsed response." That is what is so valuable about so much of popular culture—it is so "naive," so trashy, so honest and unrehearsed a response, even though, from a technical aspect, it is often sophisticated. It is American culture with its defenses down. It is the cultural equivalent of those slips of the tongue we make which, if Freud is correct, are tied to important but hidden aspects of our psyches. Celia may eat gourmet food (and speculate, endlessly, about moral philosophy and the nature of photography) but it is also important to remember, as the poet tells us, "Celia shits." We all do, which makes toilet paper a major industry.

There's Methodism to My Madness

I had written in 1980, in my book *Television as an Instrument of Terror: Essays on Media, Popular Culture and Everyday Life:*

> For the moment . . . I eschew theories of the high as well as middle range and continue to concentrate upon specific phenomena—relating them, of course, as best I can, to larger pursuits. Recall that I was the first to explain that the McDonald's hamburger chain is an evangelical religion, and the first to enunciate the notion of *Hamburgeoisement*. Remember how I showed that white bread is anti-ideological, in keeping with the American political sensibility. Don't forget that I identified the sexual identity of household appliances and explained that baseball is a kind of sexual initiation rite. Keep in mind that I was the first to discern that America was undergoing a process of *motelization*, which refers to the rapid industrialization of the household and destruction of the family unit, and that I enunciated the *Berger Hypottythesis*, which argues that the battle of the budget is connected to the toilet training of our congressmen and senators. (1980, 9,10)

I think you get the idea. More recent discoveries have taken on a more philosophical cast, as in my essay on deodorants ("I Stink, Therefore I Am") and on advertising ("To Buy Is to Be Perceived").

My interest in analyzing popular texts led me, eventually, to speculate about how it was that I found the things in them that I did. As a student asked me, after I had given a lecture on some of my admittedly preposterous notions, "How do you come up with these ideas?"

The answer is that I make use of a number of different methods of analysis. I would not describe myself as primarily a semiotician or a psychoanalytically oriented analyst, though these methodologies are found throughout my work. What I am analyzing determines what methods I use in making my analysis. Let me say something here about four of the more important methods of analysis and the work that I've done using each (or, as is most usually the case, using different methodologies in conjunction with one another).

Applied Psychoanalytic Theory

I used Freud's concepts of the id, ego, and superego to analyze *Star Trek*. I suggested each of the three main characters was one-dimensional; thus Kirk was a superego figure, Spock an ego figure, and McCoy an id figure, and the three of them added up to one person. I analyzed Dick Tracy as representing a distorted and somewhat pathological superego figure and suggested that the physical ugliness of the grotesques in the strip was a manifestation of their moral ugliness. I've also dealt with aggressive passivity in *Blondie* and the split personality in Superman and with Pac-Man as a form of auto-eroticism.

Applied Semiotic Theory

In recent years I've been drawn to semiotic theory, Proppian analysis, and related techniques to the extent that I sometimes characterize myself as a "mad binarist." I've used semiotics to analyze the famous Macintosh "1984" commercial, to explain the difference between San Francisco and Los Angeles, to analyze the pilot episode of *Cheers*, the structure of jokes, numerous films and television programs (*Upstairs, Downstairs; Paper Chase, Kung Fu, The Return of the Jedi, The Terminator*, etc.), various household objects and everyday rituals, and so on.

I might point out that, like many others, I was doing semiotic analyses before I knew what semiotics was and anything about its methodologies and concepts. I had the notion that certain interesting phenomena (comic strips, commercials, sports), were signifiers of important values and ideas and dealt with what I thought these phenomena reflected about our psyches, society, and culture.

When I was on sabbatical in England in 1973 I met Jean-Marie Benoist, who was at the time the French cultural attache to England, at a conference. We got to know each other a bit and I gave him a couple of my books to read since he was interested in the comics and popular culture. After reading them he said, "Arthur . . . you are a semiotician!" "I am?" I replied. And having been labelled one, I had no choice (so labelling theory suggests) but to become one. I was greatly encouraged when I read Barthes' *Mythologies* which uses semiotics to analyze such topics as soap advertisements, steak and chips, and other aspects of popular culture.

Applied Sociology Theory

Using what might be broadly defined as "sociological" techniques I've written about such topics as Levi's, and the nature of fashion, ethnic humor, and social class in *All in The Family*, football and baseball, advertising, and department stores as functional alternatives of cathedrals. Much of my work is sociological to the extent that it seeks to relate the object of my attention—whether a joke or a film or an artifact—to social and political considerations. My work is not empirical and would be considered "soft" (some might say "mushy") sociology or social science; but I am a critic and I am concerned with texts and how they generate meaning and not, from an empirical perspective, that is, with audiences and their opinions and attitudes as measured by instruments of one sort or another.

Applied Marxist Analysis

Marxist culture theory is so vague, in one respect, and complicated, in another, that it is hard to pin down. I would not characterize myself as a Marxist, though I do, from time to time, make use of Marxist concepts. I have written an essay "Hidden Compulsion in Television" (a rewrite and amplification of my essay "Television as an Instrument of Terror") using Marxist concepts to deal with television and society. This essay draws upon ideas found in Henry LeFebvre's *Everyday Life in the Modern World* and deals with the relation that I believe exists between alienation, consumer lust, terror and ideological domination, and television in America (as well as other societies).

I have also dealt with the symbolic significance of Daddy Warbucks in *Little Orphan Annie* and suggested that he functions as an apologist for corporate capitalism whose basic function is mystification. *Star Trek*, I pointed out, is about "enterprise" (as in "free enterprise") and could be looked upon as a morality play about the spread of American values and ideology and the fear of contamination by aliens (foreigners with strange ideas).

The problem with Marxist media and culture criticism, as argued in *Media Analysis Techniques*, is that it tends to be so doctrinaire and predictable. On the other hand, there are now many Marxists such as Haug and Enzenberger who are much more sophisticated and have interesting ideas that can be "appropriated" (a good Marxist concept).

It is unusual for me to write something that is "purely" semiotic or psychoanalytic. This is because each of these techniques often has interesting things to reveal about the object of analysis; also, the techniques are often related to one another, so it is quite natural to use a number of them. There is no royal road to analysis.

All of these methods are nonempirical, "data-free" (speaking of numerical data, that is) modes of interpretation. All of these methods define themselves as either human or social "sciences," I should point out. They all involve the application of concepts to texts, objects, phenomena, etc. and endeavor to explain their subjects. My work, for instance, is full of inferences, parallels, generalizations, and "insights." I endeavor to "see the universe in a grain of sand." There is, thus, an element of risk since I cannot "prove" (whatever that means) that my interpretations are right or worth considering. I've often said that I would rather be interesting than right; there are some who suggest I do not succeed in being either.

Much of what I do might be described as a kind of cultural anthropology for postliterate (there is some question about that matter now in America), complex societies. These methods are very much those used by literary critics and other scholars and are the focus of a lively debate in many departments. Just as anthropology has become, I feel, the most interesting of the social sciences, literary (and culture) theory has become the most interesting or "hottest" topic in literature and humanities departments. This is because, I would argue, the old techniques and methodologies don't seem to have gotten us very far.

An Overview of My Work

I have written (and in some cases edited) two books on the comics (*Li'l Abner* and *The Comic-Stripped American*), two books on popular culture (*Pop Culture, Television as an Instrument of Terror*), two methodology books (*Media Analysis Techniques, Signs in Contemporary Culture*), two books on television (*The TV-Guided American, Television in Society*), two books on media and society (*About Man: an Introduction to Anthropology, Media USA*), a book on advertising (*Semiotics and Advertising*) and a book on film (*Film in Society*).

Li'l Abner is, as I mentioned earlier, my Ph.D. dissertation and describes the methodology one might use in dealing with comics. It has chapters on the narrative structure of comics, the use of language in comics, and the visual or graphic aspect of comics. It also tied Li'l Abner to Southwestern humor and made use of psychoanalytic theory to analyze the symbolic significance of the Shmoo (suggesting it was a phallic symbol).

In *The Comic-Stripped American* I took a number of comic strips that I considered to be important and looked at them in terms of such things as heroic figures, values reflected, and allusions to social and political matters. The book covered everything from *The Yellow Kid* to underground comics and argued that "any medium that has the continued attention of hundreds of millions of people deserves serious attention and study." This notion ran counter to the notion that dominated the academy (with few exceptions) which was that if lots of people do something it is, by definition, unimportant.

I adopted the same techniques in all of my other work—that is, I took a text (comic strip, television program, television genre, artifact or whatever) and tried to "read" its social, psychological, cultural, and political significance and see what it reflected about American character, culture, and society. At times, in the earlier books, I must confess, my prose became somewhat purple, as in the last sentence in my chapter on *Dick Tracy*:

> Tracy has continued on in his relentless pursuit of crime, a servant of a stern God, in a never-ending quest for the sublimity of a community of saints.

My more recent work might be characterized as having less flamboyant language and more flamboyant analyses.

I wrote *Media Analysis Techniques* to use in a course I teach on that subject (Analysis of the Public Arts), and because I thought a primer on the basic methods of analysis might be useful to others. I had to make the book short and therefore wrote in a very compressed manner and made extensive use of quotations to give students the central concepts in semiotics, psychoanalytic theory, Marxist thought, and sociology—as they applied to media and culture criticism.

I also provided essays in the second half of the book in which I showed readers how the concepts in the first half might be applied. In the original version of the book I wrote four different analyses of fashion, but my editor felt I needed to focus directly on media; so I wrote four new chapters on fashion advertising, *Murder on the Orient Express*, football, and all-news radio. A friend of mine, a mass-communications scholar from Korea, made an amusing comment after the book was published. "Who would ever think that *you* would write a book on methodology!"

I found this comment interesting for two reasons. First, it has to do with my "public" persona as a cartoonist and humorist, a punster and gagster, an amusing but presumably not serious fellow, a "wild analyst." (I once suggested in a lecture that to be a "wild analyst" two things are very helpful—to have tenure and to be a full professor.) Methodology books are to be written by "serious scholars" and, one might suppose, dreary souls who cannot do "research." Those who can do research do research; those who can't do research write methodology books. Those who can't write methodology books write textbooks. Those who can't write textbooks become committee members and campus politicos.

Second, there seems to be an element of guilt by association. If you work with trash, with subliterary materials, your analyses must be (apodictically speaking) intuitive, subjective, superficial. The mass media and popular culture do not have "prestige" and are not considered serious subjects by many scholars. People assume, I imagine, that you work with these materials because you like them, for one reason or another. (This logic suggests that sociologists do research in bars because they like to drink and oncologists like cancer.) And it also assumes that those who work with popular materials use no methods. Anything goes!

I must confess to having written about my work (trying to be facetious, without success it seems) that "I make it up as I go along and throw in charts from time to time to make sociologists happy." But, in fact, I cannot imagine anyone analyzing any text or anything else without some methodology, even though this may not be fully conscious or worked out. All criticism implies some kind of a point of view, some way of making sense of things. The question is, what methods are most appropriate and interesting for the phenomenon, topic, or text being analyzed?

My book on semiotic methods, *Signs in Contemporary Culture*, was written to be an introductory textbook, which would explain a concept from semiotics and then show how the concept could be applied. Instead of dividing the book into halves, as I did with *Media Analysis Techniques*, I divided the chapters into halves. My editor decided the book should be marketed as a professional book so instead of the book costing ten or twelve dollars it ended up costing more than thirty dollars. What is interesting is that the book comes directly out of one of my journals.

After returning from England and a course of reading books on semiotics, I devoted one of my journals to semiotics and called the journal "The Sign." I then spent a few weeks brainstorming on signs, speculating about every aspect of signs I could think of. I produced a number of pages in which I took a general topic and then listed things I could use to flesh out the topic. I saw the book as an original and even idiosyncratic introduction to semiotics, yet when it was reveiwed the general thrust of the reviews was "he covers all the conventional topics." I found that amusing.

I have edited a book that is my first *mainstream* text—*Media USA*— and would like to say something about what I tried to do in the book. I say mainstream because my other books were written or edited for smaller audiences and what might be described as tributary courses. This book was primarily designed for those large "introduction to mass communications" lecture courses that are offered by most communications departments, though it has been used for many other purposes.

Editing the book was a fascinating (if exhausting) experience because I had the obligation, I felt, to offer a "picture" of what I thought media studies should be like. The book had to be comprehensive and deal with the topics that are generally covered in such courses—and it había to be interesting so students would read it. I had examined a number of readers and, for one reason or another, did not like them. I thought much of the material was dry and uninteresting, with too much emphasis on the press and legal matters. So my task, as I saw it, was to put together a book that was entertaining (in the most positive sense of the word) and authoritative.

I tried to do this by enticing a number of people (many from the media) to write original articles for me and by finding work by outstanding scholars that were accessible to young students. I also decided to offer an innovation and to write substantial introductions to each essay which were not, for the most part, recapitulations of the main points made in each article. This allowed me to deal with tangential ideas, to offer quotations that were relevant and to carry on a dialogue, of sorts, with the essays. In addition, I wrote introductions for each of the sections of the book. Thus I wrote about one hundred pages in *Media USA* (not including two of my articles), so that my presence in the book is substantial.

I also wrote a teacher's manual that offers a number of projects and activities for students as well as provides the required study and discussion questions and exam questions. My editor displayed a great deal of courage in asking me to do the book, for just as one friend never thought I'd do a methodology book, I'm sure others thought I'd never do a media reader. And that is because I'm seen by them, I would imagine, as too marginal a scholar, one who writes only impressionistic think pieces and perhaps is too much involved in popular culture to be able to break away from it and do something that people teaching mass communications courses would find useful.

When people ask what my field is, I no longer say "popular culture." One reason is that I'm not sure anyone knows, for sure, what popular culture is, and another reason is that I'm tired of trying to explain to people what I think popular culture is and what I do. So now I say "I'm a media analyst" and that seems to satisfy them. They know what the mass media are and generally feel that, somehow, they are important, and the term "analyst" suggests something scholarly and perhaps even intellectual (as opposed to "critic" which has combinations of journalism or negativity).

My most recent book is *Seeing Is Believing: An Introduction to Visual Communication*. It is an introduction to the subject which deals with the psychology of perception, the rules or basic elements of composition and design, and analyses of distinctive aspects of the media: photography, television, film, comics and cartoons, print, etc. The book also makes use of some semiotic theory and is full of my drawings and many other images from the various media.

My original goal was to provide an inexpensive book that could be used in many courses as a supplement and that would offer students that "visual literacy" that many communications scholars feel our students should have. It has been a difficult chore to keep this thin book from becoming a fat one, but I think I've succeeded. The cost, of course, is that I couldn't discuss some topics that some reviewers felt I should deal with. Some reviewers also took objection to my writing in the first person and felt that this suggested the book would be too casual and not scholarly. Thus I was forced to make some cosmetic changes, here and there, in the writing.

Personally, I see nothing wrong with using "I" in writing; it is the quality of the thinking and research that is important, not the use of pronouns. But, like any writer, I have to consider the mindset of those who might adopt and use the book and so I eliminated most of the "I's" in the manuscript. I don't think this changed the impact of my style of writing.

Current Projects

I have a number of books that I'm trying to get published. One is *Anatomy of Humor*, a collection of essays on humor, some previously published and some unpublished. Over the years I've written a good deal on this subject, which has always interested me, and I think I've made an original contribution to the analysis of humor in an unpublished "Glossary of the Techniques of Humor," which is a monograph of some sixty pages. For some reason it is hard to get books on humor published; trade publishers want books that are full of humorous material (I think mine is but they don't seem to agree) and textbook publishers don't see a market for such books.

I have another book, somewhat different from my usual work, which takes Mircea Eliade's notions, as expressed in *The Sacred and the Profane*, and applies them to American culture. It deals with three "mythic" American culture heroes—the puritan, the pioneer, and the plutocrat—and is very much an "American Studies" kind of book (whatever that means).

My interest in everyday life led me to write a short (and admittedly far out) book called *Ulysses Sociologica: Bloom's Morning*. For years I had the idea of analyzing everything that happened in a one day of a typical American's life (hence *Ulysses*) from a psychoanalytic, socio-logical, anthropological perspective (hence the *Sociologica*). I wrote a series of thirty-five or so microessays on all of the objects and activities of this typical American, one Leopold Bloom, from the time he was wakened by his clock radio to the time he had breakfast. Writing this was so exhausting, and the chances of getting the book published so remote I felt, that I decided to deal only with the morning activities.

The book deals with the significance of such topics as gel toothpaste, designer sheets, king-sized beds, slippers, pajamas, bacon and eggs, etc. It is by far my most imaginative (if you get what I mean) effort as I attempted, by sheer force of will, to wring meaning from the super-mundane aspects of our daily life.

To give you a taste of this book, let me quote from my chapter on the stocking:

> If the foot has an erotic component to it, and, in fact, often functions as a phallus, then stockings have a significance that becomes quite obvious now. If their function is to mediate, to protect the foot, and to contain body excretions, is it not possible to see putting on a stocking as being similar to putting on a condom.

Finally, there is a book I wrote which is a collection of some twenty simulations, activities, exercises and games that I invented. They are designed to be used in courses dealing with media, criticism, and culture studies. I developed these games over a number of years and find they help my students learn to apply concepts (as contrasted with merely understanding them).

I hope by now that my readers have a pretty good sense of my interests and the work I've done—my research program. Now I would like to characterize my work and say something about the difficulties some people have with it.

Methodological Problematics

In this section I will deal with some of the criticisms that have been made, or might be made, of my research program. Earlier I suggested that all critics and analysts have a point of view and use various methods or perspectives in their work, whether they are aware of it or not. There is always, then, methodology to be considered, whether one is discussing an experiment or culture criticism. What methods are used? How legitimate are they? How well are they applied? What assumptions does the researcher hold? How valid are they? What kind of "proof" is offered? Do any interesting generalizations emerge from the research? What evidence supports these generalizations? How important is the topic being analyzed?

I will now list and discuss some of the major problems which I surmise others have—or might have—with my work.

My work is Hyper-Eclectic

Let me quote a passage from John Dryden's "Absalom and Achitophel" (1681) that is relevant here:

. . . a man so various that he seem'd to be

Not one, but all mankind's epitome:

Stiff in opinions, always in the wrong,

Was ev'rything by starts, and nothing long;

But, in the course of one revolving moon

Was chemist, fiddler, statesman, and buffoon;

Then all for women, painting, rhyming, drinking,

Besides ten thousand freaks that died in thinking.

Like the victim of this poem, it might be suggested that I have no research program, per se, and merely write on whatever topics interest me. When I was an undergraduate, one of my professors said "The trouble with you, Berger, is that you want to jump on a horse and ride off in all directions at the same time!"

I don't think that I am "hyper-eclectic" at all. If you look at all the books and articles I've written, you can see that they deal with some aspect of popular culture, the mass media, or everyday life. Years ago George Gerbner suggested to me that my field is "communications" which is itself often held to be hyper-eclectic or so broad a field as to cover almost everything. From my perspective, and this is reflected in my text *Media Analysis Techniques*, communications is a field that is open to research from people in all the disciplines. If you look at the kind of research that is published in most of the scholarly journals in communications (if that is not an oxymoron), it is often discipline-based—sociological, social-psychological, economic, etc.

I might also argue that popular culture and media studies is so broad a field and so dynamic a subject area that covering it is Sisyphean. As soon as you analyze one text or genre or phenomena you find countless others to occupy your attention. So you have to learn to be selective. And since I keep a journal, my "ten thousand freaks" don't die in the thinking. They are recorded in my journals and often end up in my books and articles.

My Work Is Interpretative.

Of course it is, I would say, and why not? I see nothing wrong with "interpretation," and, as a matter of fact, I don't know how anyone can avoid it. Even the most rigorously designed experiment yields results that have to be interpreted. (This means if, for one reason or another, you want to take issue with some research, and you can't fault the design, you can always find problems with the interpretation. If you have difficulties here, too, you must take recourse in saying that the topics are uninteresting and trivial, the conclusions or generalizations that emerge from the research are unsurprising, or that the problem is theoretically uninteresting.)

Much of my work involves trying to make sense of texts—of specific works such as an episode of *Cheers*, a commercial, a series or an artifact. I try to figure out how people read or find meaning in these texts and to suggest how the values and beliefs reflected in them relate to the social and political order. Semiotic theory has suggested, remember, that people do not all "decode" text the same way and that there are many aberrant decodings; this calls into question the utility of content analysis, which assumes that audiences decode texts the same way sociologists do.

Too much work in communications is based on social-psychology and what I would describe, to use Dewey's language, as "the quest for certainty." And much of this social-psychological research is ill-conceived, spurious, trivial, or all three. It focuses on audiences and ignores *what* the audiences are hearing or watching.

The focus on meaning in texts requires, I submit, interpretation, which must be evaluated, then, on the face-value of the argument made and the reasonableness of the generalizations (about what the text reveals about social and political matters) that follow from the interpretation.

There is the "hocus-pocus versus God's truth" problem to be considered. Is what I find in a text something that is actually in the text (God's truth) or a figment of my often fertile imagination (hocus pocus)? That, I submit, is up to my reader to determine. I operate on the assumption that what I find in a text is actually there, and my function is to reveal things hidden in texts that help us see them in a new and more profound light. The fact that other critics may interpret the same text in a different manner is no different, if you think about it, from the fact that economists (generally considered to be the most "scientific" of the social-scientists) from different schools of economics interpret the same data in different ways.

The model for much of my work comes from cultural anthropology and the process of argumentation and legitimation are the same. If an anthropologist were to be parachuted down into some preliterate tribe and spend a couple of years with them, recording their myths and legends, finding out about their heroes and gods, analyzing their songs, their daily rituals, their foods, and their attitudes, nobody would think twice about it. But if you do the same things with American culture, it is considered, somehow, a trivial pursuit and not worthy of the academy. Considered by whom we might ask? Those in the so-called prestige disciplines? Or what once were the prestige disciplines? Those that are "really" scientific? I think things are changing now, and indeed we now see anthropologists turning their attention to American culture in increasing numbers with extremely interesting results.

My Work Is Full of Preposterous Ideas.

Actually, I've never been able to publish some of the most preposterous of my ideas, so those who think that my "Evangelical Hamburger" notion is bizarre have been spared notions that are even harder to digest or take seriously. Thus my essay "ErosGOPanalia or the Berger Hypottythesis" (in which I argue that Republican fiscal conservatives are anal erotics who have transferred their obsession with holding back their stools to the economic realm) has never been published. I sent it, for the fun of it, to a very distinguished economics journal and received the following reply:

> Dear Prof. Berger:
> Thank you for sending your essay "ErosGOPanalia" for consideration. The editors have decided that your essay is not suitable for publication in our journal . . . or in any that we can conceive of.

I have other "preposterous" ideas as well. For example, it seems to me that the reason we like blondes with dark tans is that we can have the best of both worlds in the same woman: the cold, Nordic, not-to-be-touched white woman and the hot-blooded and sexually explosive dark woman. (These are, it has been suggested, dominant stereotypes in American culture.) It also seems to me that those advertisements showing cars bursting through cardboard signs are, ultimately, metaphors reflecting the defloration of virgins by men with penises of iron (that is new cars). "A hard man," as they say, "is good to find."

There are, I would say, two "subtexts" to this criticism of my work as having "preposterous" ideas. *There is the suggestion that I misapply concepts (whose validity is questionable in the first place).* I am willing to take a concept for a ride, to follow it where it leads me, without much thought or concern about whether the results are absurd and ridiculous. If you take a far-out concept and misapply it, or use it loosely if you want to be nice, you end up with nonsense. Even if you don't misapply it you end up with nonsense, many would argue.

I happen to believe (perhaps being "overly defensive" for those who accept psychoanalytic thought) that so-called nonsense and preposterous ideas have more to tell us, often, than conventional wisdom and accepted truths and methodologies. Any reasonably intelligent individual can be taught the conventional social-scientific methodologies and do decent enough research. But how many people can come up with really preposterous ideas (especially in a post-modern society)?

The second subtext here is that *I don't take research, social science, the intellectual life (or whatever) "seriously."* I am more interested, this argument suggests, in making a good play on words or coming up with an amusing idea than anything else. Thus I am a poor representative of the academy and discredit, by my actions, all those who are seriously committed to research. As a colleague of mine (not from my department) once put it, "Arthur, you're a social scientist, but you're not a *good* social scientist." At that time I had published six books and he had published one essay, from his dissertation. "Says who?" I replied.

It is my insouciance that disturbs some academics who are terribly serious about their work, which gives them a sense of importance. *Their* lives are not "minor events in the ongoing universe." (I have generally found the best scholars to be the most humorous, least solemn ones, but my sample may be too limited.) The fact is I do clown around a lot; if there is methodism to my madness, there is madness to my method.

In *Zen and the Comic Spirit* Conrad Hyers lists a number of techniques used by the Zen masters which helps explain what I am up to with all my nonsense:

A glance at some of the common features of comic lines, behaviour or situations reveals the close analogy between comic techniques and Zen techniques, as well as the serviceability of comic techniques in Zen: irrationality, contradiction, incongruity, absurdity, irrelevancy, triviality, nonsense, distortion, abruptness, shock, sudden twist, reversal or overturning. In both comedy and Zen one is prevented from drawing a purely intellectual conclusion at the end of an argument and therefore entering the abstractness and deceptiveness of a pseudo-appropriation of the truth. (Hyers, p. 142)

The Zen masters, Hyers points out, often took the *pose* of fools and clowns, sometimes dressing in tattered clothing and shoes too large for their feet.

My method, like the Zen masters, is to use indirection; when I use humor (and I don't use it all the time by any means) it is to facilitate learning, to confront readers with alien ideas which force them, I hope, to see things in new ways and to question the way they have made sense of the world.

I use humor and absurdity when I teach (and, when possible, when I lecture). Laughter, I believe, cushions and eases the "shock of recognition" we often experience when we suddenly see something in a new way. And the notion that there is generally more than meets the eye is central to my thinking.

My Work Makes Use of Psychoanalytic concepts.

Reviewers of my work never tire of quoting Freud's remark that "sometimes a cigar is only a cigar," which suggests, also, that sometimes a cigar *isn't* only a cigar. The implication is that I find phallic symbols everywhere and distort what many consider to be the already highly suspect Freudian theories by my excesses.

I would argue that when I use Freudian analyses I do so with a good deal of caution and generally have what I consider to be a reasonable argument to make. There is a tendency for many scholars to dismiss Freudian and psychoanalytic thought as unscientific and absurd. The question I always ask when I apply Freudian thought to a text is, "why is it that psychoanalytic concepts seem to do such a good job of explaining what happens?"

In recent years, psychoanalytic thought (in combination with semiotics and Marxism) has made a comeback in France and other continental countries, so I expect that it will only be a matter of time before it is fashionable here again. The dominant figures in literary theory and culture theory (and even in the social sciences, I might add) tend to be continental—Lévi-Strauss, Barthes, Lacan, Gadamer, Lotman, Foucault, Saussure, Derrida—most of whom use some combination of semiotic, Marxist, and Freudian thought in their work.

I can expect, then, to find my Freudianism (and perhaps my work, in general) "fashionable" in the not-too-distant future—if I stick to my "guns." Am I deluded? Am I being too defensive?

My Pose of Nonseriousness Works Too Well.

I may be, I must confess, exaggerating the comedic aspects of my work and personality. If you read my work you do not find that much clowning around. It is the Freudianism which, more than anything else, I suspect, has given people the notion that my work lacks the higher seriousness. That, and the fact that my lectures and presentations are often humorous. The fact that I like a good laugh and like to write an occasional zany piece (and have made light of the way I work) has led some people to stereotype me, I fear. On my campus people know me as "the comics man," though I've hardly written anything on the comics for fifteen years.

My Work Is Not Research.

Is it possible that this essay on my research program is being written by a person who doesn't have a *program* and who doesn't conduct *research*? That would be a fine kettle of fish. A colleague of mine was kidding me about my productivity. "How do you do it, Arthur?" he said. "But, then, you just make it all up, you don't do *research!*" It all depends, of course, on how you define research. If research involves controlled experiments, some form of quantitative data-gathering, etc. I don't do research. But neither, then, do most historians, literary scholars, political theorists, social theorists . . . I could go on and on.

If you define research as using resources, such as applying the ideas and writings of others, to my investigations, then I do qualify as a researcher. My research is qualitative rather than quantitative, as I try to interpret and understand texts and other phenomena. If you look through my writings you see a large number of quotations, often from continental sources, for it is elite continental literary and cultural thought that I have applied to my subliterary and subcultural subjects. (I sometimes think I have the mind of a Frenchman imprisoned in the body of an American.)

My Subjects Are Trivial and What I Study is Junk.

Popular culture is, for the most part, full of junk, what sometimes I call "significant trivia." But just as a slip of the tongue may be, in itself, trivial, it may signify and reveal important things. I have already discussed this matter in this chapter. If you look at things from a semiotic perspective and don't get hung up about the aesthetic quality of your texts, popular culture and the popular arts provide signifiers of great resonance. Simple works can reflect complicated matters.

It could even be argued that "simple" texts and phenomena pose more of a problem for the analyst than "complex" ones. It isn't too difficult to find "important" matters to discuss in great works of art (though our assessment of what works are great and not so great seem to change with remarkable rapidity), but to find them in something simple and trivial is an accomplishment.

There is a halo effect for those who work on important problems and topics that must be considered, a kind of "gilt" by association. Those who do this work often develop a certain kind of presence, one that I would describe as "high seriousness." Unfortunately, what you often find is that the higher the seriousness and the more "important" the topic, the less one finds in the way of actual accomplishments. (At the conferences I attend I am often amazed by the level of research and amount of work so many people say they are doing. I never seem to have serious issues to deal with or important topics under research; instead, I fool around with whatever it is that interests me and usually it is pretty silly stuff. I used to think that all graduate students should take a seminar in "deportment and the projection of high seriousness" but I now feel they pick it up on their own, very nicely.)

I am very latitudinarian about research programs. Let people investigate whatever they want. What bothers me is when people in the academy, with what seems to me to be an elitist bias, devalue the areas that I and others work in—popular culture, the mass media, and everyday life. I think the quality of one's work should be the issue, not the area in which one chooses to work. If popular culture and everyday life was good enough for Roland Barthes, it should be good enough for anyone. (Ironically, when I've been in Europe, I found that intellectuals and scholars there were much more positive about this kind of research than they are here in America.) I think this is changing, fortunately.

I should confess, here, that I have used popular culture as a means of "sugar coating the didactic pill." By dealing with popular materials in my writing and in my teaching I am able to sneak in discussions of issues and topics and theories that otherwise would turn off many of my readers and students. Popular culture is a Trojan horse, used to breach the walls of indifference in many of my students (who are taking "required" courses) and others, as well.

My Writing is Too Easy To Read and May Be Mere Journalism.

This criticism suggests that my writing style accurately, and perhaps unconsciously, reflects the level and seriousness of my analyses. In effect I have violated the canons of scholarship by adopting (in many cases, that is) a breezy style, full of wordplay, snide remarks about universities and professors, opinions, and wild generalizations.

I'm not sure where to draw the line between scholarly writing and journalism. In Europe, there is a tradition of scholars writing for newspapers and magazines. When they do so does that mean what they write is less serious? I've always felt it was the quality of one's thought and ideas that is important, and not your style of writing or where you publish.

Personally speaking I don't like to write in a formal style, which one finds in many scholarly journals. But when I write for "serious" publications, my writing is similar in style to that of the other writers. My stylistic excesses generally only occur in situations where I feel they are useful: an occasional article or chapter in a book where I offer a "far-fetched" idea or so. Sometimes my students suggest I am "far out." I argue that being far out is relative to where one starts, and it may be that they (and others) are really "far in."

I wrote a book *Seeing Is Believing: An Introduction to Visual Communication*, and as I mentioned earlier, I had to change the style because many of the readers who evaluated the manuscript felt that textbooks must be written in the third person. It wasn't a big issue for me, but I think it might be salutory if textbooks had a bit more personality, vitality, and authorial signature to them. I realize that textbooks are supposed to be summaries of the basic principles of a subject, but all writing involves a matter of selection (what to include, what to leave out), so that even textbooks are much more "personal" than they seem to be.

Since I am writing this for a scholarly publication I probably should have taken advantage of the situation to write in a solemn and (even better) obscure manner. The French are supreme at writing unintelligibly, though Germans, Russians, and other Continentals do a pretty good job at it, also. There seems to be a correlation between status with intellectuals and the scholarly community in America and opaqueness. I am not talking about the dull, plodding prose one finds in sociology journals and the like but truly inspired non-readability.

My N = 1.

I confess, that unlike Piaget, whose N was 2 or 3 (or something like that), my N = 1. What does this mean? That my focus is on my observations, my interpretations, my insights, my conclusions and not on making studies of audiences, groups, etc. that would yield suitably large and respectable Ns. But just as you don't go to an eye doctor to have a broken ankle repaired, you shouldn't come to me if you want quantitative studies of public opinion, attitude change, etc. (There are, of course, some scholars who believe that only quantitative research is acceptable; anything else becomes a matter of opinion. I have already dealt with this.)

I might put it this way, "the N justifies the means."

My Productivity Suggests My Work Can't Be Any Good.

Sour grapes, I say. Could empirically based scholars legitimately make generalizations like this? I doubt it. This argument suggests that anyone who writes a great deal can't do quality work, which would malign the work of many outstanding scholars such as Aaron Wild-avsky who have been extraordinarily productive. My productivity is connected to several things: I have a lot of ideas, I am very disciplined, I work hard when I get involved with a project, and I type fast.

A colleague of mine (not in my department), who prided himself on his powers of analysis and his empiricism, once said to me, "All of your books are unpublishable!" He suggested that my books had been published because, somehow, I had been able to "dupe" editors into putting my stuff out and that my work did not deserve to be published. He also explained to me that his work (and the work of certain of his colleagues) was "too good to be published." Those are the precise words he used; I am not making this up, though this story makes you understand why it is often very hard to take scholars and academic life seriously.

And that is where we left things. He and many of his colleagues continue to do work—I don't think they actually write anything to speak of—that is, "too good to be published" (though they once decided they would regard dittoed papers, departmental memos, etc. as the equivalent of publications, refereeing, I assume, one another's efforts) and I have continued to dupe unsuspecting and naive editors into publishing my "unpublishable" articles, monographs and books.

I think that this chapter—or is it a confessional—does a good job of giving my readers a sense of my interests, thinking, my writing style, my personality and what I see as the main difficulties or problematics (I was tempted to say "problem-antics") with my work. These problematics, I might add, are ones that I assume others might find or have found with my work. There are, I know, a number of people who are interested in what I do and like what I write, some of whom are kind enough to read my books or to use my books in the courses. What I have been offering is what might be described as a "worst case scenario," and I may have been too hard on myself. Some would say, "impossible."

A Researcher without Quantities Quotes
from *a Man Without Qualities*

What of my plans for the future? Let me quote here from Robert Musil's book, *The Man Without Qualities*:

> . . . by the time they have reached the middle of their life's journey few people remember how they have managed to arrive at themselves, at their amusements, their point of view, their wife, character, occupation and successes, but they cannot help feeling that not much is likely to change any more. It might even be asserted that they have been cheated, for one can nowhere discover any sufficient reason for everything's having come about as it has. It might just as well have turned out differently.

In a sense, I think Musil is right, for I cannot see any major changes taking place in my research program, though it may be that small changes, over the years, add up to substantial changes. When I was in the eleventh grade, one of my teachers told me I was an iconoclast, which suggests to me that even when young I had a stance, a perspective on things that has probably informed much of my work. (To what degree does personality shape one's research and one's career? This question always intrigues me.)

Let me say something about future projects. My first task—and it is a never-ending chore—is to get my past projects (that is, my books and articles) published. The more I publish, the harder it is to get anything else published, or so it often seems. Thus a good deal of my life is spent on "marketing" work I already have done. And I am always somewhat anxious about undertaking a new project since I wonder whether I'll end up with just one more unpublishable book or article.

On the other hand, nobody can expect to bat 1000, and I generally write because I want to know what I think about some topic that interests me, and the only way I can find out is to write about it. This forces me to come to conclusions and also leads to insights about things that I hadn't had when I started writing. The process of writing always leads me to new discoveries. In looking through my journals I notice that I seem to depend as much time "doing my crazy dance" with editors as I do speculating about topics that interest me.

I have reviewed books for *The Journal of Communication* regularly, and generally I have chosen the books I review. Recently I've reviewed two books by the German Marxist Wolfgang Haug on commodity aesthetics, and this got me interested in the "coercive" power of style and aesthetics on individuals and societies. I may pursue this topic if I can find a way to deal with it.

I'm also more and more interested in humor and will continue to work in that area. In recent years humor has attracted a lot of scholarly attention from people in many disciplines and in all areas of the world, which means that there is now that critical mass that tends to legitimate research on any topic. Much of my research has involved humor. My dissertation was on humor and many chapters in my books on comics and television dealt with humor. My interest in humor as a scholar may be connected with the fact that I am a humorous person and am curious about myself. In investigating humor I'll probably find out something about myself.

I've written humorous poetry (even have had poems published in *The New York Times* and *Saturday Review of Literature*). I developed a form of the Clerihew based on people's names such as:

Dame May/ Was witty
But John Greanleaf/ Was Whittier.

Aga Khan
But Immanuel/ Kant.

Oscar/ Was Wilde
But Thornton/ Was Wilder

Recently I started publishing a comic newsletter, full of crazy articles, comic poems, etc. which I put out sporadically and send to various friends.

And of course, I will continue to analyze texts (television shows, films, commercials, etc.) objects, and practices that get my attention and seem worth investigating. That is par for the course. From time to time, also, I am asked to write something for a publication. This always intrigues me because I tend to see my work as somewhat marginal, offbeat, and opposed to the dominant research paradigms.

On the other hand, I also think that things may change and the kind of work I've done may come to be seen as an approach to be used along with the more traditional approaches.

A number of years ago George Gerbner asked me to write an essay on popular culture for *The Journal of Communication*. I wrote a long essay, of perhaps thirty pages, with a long ''social-scientific'' title, which he cut down to about five pages. He used one section of the essay, titled ''The Secret Agent,'' in the Spring, 1974 issue of the journal. In the essay I explained that people who investigate popular culture are (like) secret agents, who look for all the ''secrets'' hidden in the culture around them. I drew a picture of myself as a secret agent, which he used. And that led to my eventually adopting the persona of the secret agent.

Recruited by George Gerbner, who was, I understand, connected in some way to espionage himself, I became a self-styled secret agent and have spent my academic career looking for hidden meanings and latent functions and all kinds of other things. The problem with secret agents is, as we all know, you never can tell when the information they provide you is reliable. Some secret agents are double agents and some secret agents aren't very good secret agents. Caveat emptor.

Thus, I expect to continue writing works that some people will describe as merely "pointing out what is obvious to everyone" and others will describe as "far out and ridiculous." Since you can't please everyone, you might as well please yourself, and that is what I've done over the years.

An Anecdote on the Literary Life

A number of years ago I was invited to a party that was given by two literary agents in San Francisco. The room was crowded with writers and would-be writers, some of whom I knew and others who I'd never seen before. A young woman, seeing I was alone, came over to me.

"Are you *literary*?" she asked.

"Yes," I replied.

"Have you published?" she asked.

"Yes," I replied.

"Fiction?" she asked.

"A lot of people think so," I replied.

Bibliography

Bagdikian, Ben H. Summer 1985. "The U.S. Media: Supermarket or Assembly Line." *Journal of Communication*.

Ball-Rokeach, Sandra and Muriel G. Cantor, eds. 1986. *Media, Audience and Social Structure*. Newbury Park, CA: Sage Publications.

Barthes, Roland. 1972. *Mythologies*. New York: Hill & Wang.

Berger, Arthur Asa. 1970. *Li'l Abner: A Study in American Satire*. New York: Twayne Publishers.

Berger, Arthur Asa. 1973. *The Comic-Stripped American*. New York: Walker & Co.

Berger, Arthur Asa. 1975. *The TV-Guided American*. New York: Walker & Co.

Berger, Arthur Asa. 1980. *Television as an Instrument of Terror*. New Brunswick, NJ: Transaction Books.

Berger, Arthur Asa. 1982. *Media Analysis Techniques*. Beverly Hills, CA: SAGE Publications.

Berger, Arthur Asa. 1988. *Media USA: Process and Effect*. White Plains, NY: Longman.

Berger, Arthur Asa, ed. 1988. *Television in SOCIETY*. New Brunswick, NJ: Transaction Books.

Berger, Arthur Asa, ed. 1989. *Political Culture and Public Opinion*. New Brunswick, NJ: Transaction Books.

Berger, Arthur Asa. 1989. *Seeing Is Believing: An Introduction to Visual Communication*. Mountain View, CA: Mayfield Publishing Co.

Berger, John. 1972. *Ways of Seeing*. London: Penguin Books.

Deutsch, Karl W. 1966. *The Nerves of Government: Models of Political Communication and Control*. New York: Free Press.

Douglas, Mary. 1973. *Natural Symbols*. New York: Vintage Books.

Douglas, Mary. 1982. *In the Active Voice*. London: Routledge & Kegan Paul.

Douglas, Mary and Aaron Wildavsky. 1982. *Risk and Culture*. Berkeley, Univ. of California Press.

Dundes, Alan. 1987. *Cracking Jokes: Studies of Sick Humor Cycles and Stereotypes*. Berkeley: Ten Speed Press.

Durkheim, Emile. 1965. *The Elementary Forms of Religious Life*. New York: The Free Press.

Fiske, John. 1982. *Introduction to Communication Studies*. London: Methuen.

Freud, Sigmund. 1930. *Civilization and Its Discontents*. London: Hogarth Press.

Freud, Sigmund. 1953. *A General Introduction to Psychoanalysis*. Garden City, NY: Permabooks.

Freud, Sigmund. 1963. *Jokes and Their Relation to The Unconscious*. New York: W.W.Norton.

Fry, William F. 1963. *Sweet Madness: A Study of Humor*. Palo Alto, CA: Pacific Books.

Fry, William F. 1975. "The Impact of Mirth and Humor." From remarks at the American Psychological Association, Sept. 3, Chicago.

Gottdiener, Mark. March 1985. "Hegemony and Mass Culture: A Semiotic Approach." *American Journal of Sociology*. Vol. 90, No.5.

Grotjahn, Martin. 1970. "Jewish Jokes and Their Relation To Masochism." In *A Celebration of Laughter*.

Hobbes, Thomas. Quoted on p. 160 in R. Piddington, 1963. *The Psychology of Laughter*. New York: Gamut.

Hyers, Conrad. 1974. *Zen and The Comic Spirit*. Philadelphia: Westminster Press.

Katz, Elihu. 1987. "On Conceptualizing Media Effects: Another Look." Reprinted in Berger, Arthur Asa. *Media USA: Process and Effect*. 1988. White Plains, NY: Longman, Inc.

Kottak, Conrad, ed. 1982. *Researching American Culture*. Ann Arbor, MI: Univ. of Michigan Press.

Leonard, George. 1968. *Education and Ecstasy*. New York: Delta Books.

Leonard, George. 1984. Personal communication. Oct. 15, 1985. Mill Valley, CA.

Lipset, Seymour Martin., ed. 1969. *Politics and the Social Sciences*. New York: Oxford Univ. Press.

McCormack, Thelma. 1986. "Reflections on the Lost Vision of Communication Theory." In Ball-Rokeach, Sandra and Muriel Cantor, eds. *Media, Audience and Social Structure*. 1986. Newbury Park, CA: Sage Publications.

Mendel, Werner W.,ed. 1970. *A Celebration of Laughter*. Los Angeles: Mara Books.

Musil, Robert. 1965. *The Man Without Qualities*. New York: Capricorn Books.

Peirce, C. S. 1977. Quoted in Sebeok, Thomas A., ed. *A Perfusion of Signs*. Bloomington, IN: 1977.

Popper, Karl and John C. Eccles. 1977. *The Self and Its Brain*. New York: Springer-Verlag.

Powell, Chris and George E.C. Paton, eds. 1988. *Humor in Society: Resistance and Control*. New York: St. Martin's Press.

Rosen, R.D. 1977. *Psychobabble*. New York: Atheneum.

Saussure, Ferdinand de. 1966. *Course in General Linquistics*. New York: McGraw-Hill Book Co.

Wildavsky, Aaron. 1984. *The Nursing Father: Moses as a Political Leader*. University, AL: Univ. of Alabama Press.

Wildavsky, Aaron. 1982. "Conditions for Pluralist Democracy: Or Cultural Pluralism Means More Than One Political Culture in a Country." Survey Research Center, Univ. of California, Berkeley.

Wildavsky, Aaron. Undated. "Choosing Preferences by Constructing Institutions: A Cultural Theory of Preference Formation." Survey Research Center, Univ. of California, Berkeley.

Zborowski, Mark and Elizabeth Herzog. 1952. *Life is With People: The Culture of the Shtetl*. New York: Schocken Books.

Name Index

Subject Index

DATE DUE